Scott Foresman - Addison Wesley

MATH

AUTHORS

Randall I. Charles

Dinah Chancellor Debbie Moore Jane F. Schielack John Van de Walle

Carne S. Barnett • Diane J. Briars • Dwight A. Cooley • Warren D. Crown
Lalie Harcourt • Martin L. Johnson • Steven J. Leinwand • Ricki Wortzman

S F
A W

Scott Foresman
Addison Wesley

Editorial Offices: Menlo Park, California • Glenview, Illinois
Sales Offices: Reading, Massachusetts • Atlanta, Georgia • Glenview, Illinois
Carrollton, Texas • Menlo Park, California

http://www.sf.aw.com

ISBN 0-201-69010-1

9 10-WC-01 00 99

Position and Classification

Theme: Celebrate Kindergarten   1

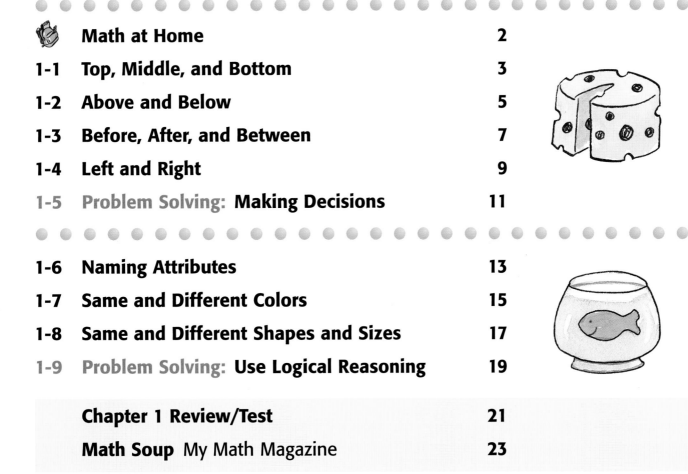

CHAPTER 2

Sort and Graph
Theme: All About Me   25

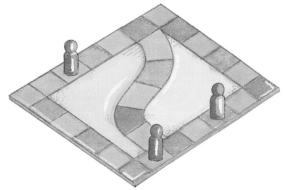

Explore Patterns

Theme: Looking for Changes   47

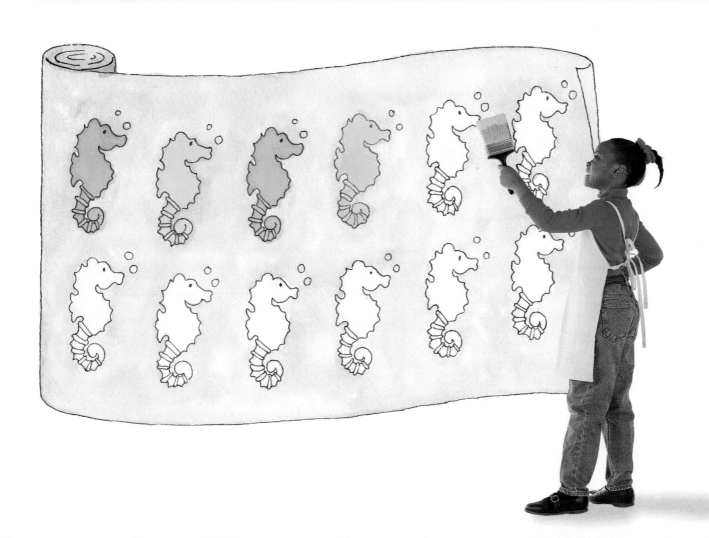

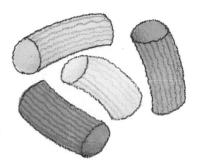

CHAPTER 4

Explore Numbers to 5
Theme: Families and Friends   67

Numbers to 10
Theme: Good Night   97

 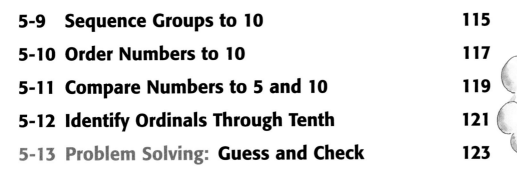

Measurement
Theme: Differences   129

Solids, Shapes, and Sharing
Theme: The Foods We Eat   153

Number Sense
Theme: Just for Fun   181

Time and Money
Theme: In the Neighborhood 207

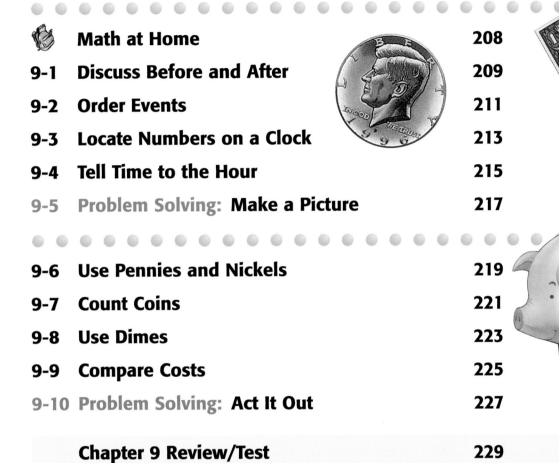

Explore Actions with Numbers

Theme: Wonderful Water 233

Larger Numbers
Theme: Kindergarten Ecology 255

Explore Addition and Subtraction
Theme: World of Animals   279

Position and Classification

Celebrate Kindergarten

Notes for Home: Your child described things in the kindergarten classroom pictured above.
Home Activity: Make a stack of objects, and ask your child to point out a red object and the top object.

Dear Family,
We will be learning words that help us describe things and words that tell where things are. I can practice by playing a game of I Spy. Here is what we can do:

> I spy something red and round.

You be the spy.
Secretly choose a thing in the room.
Tell me one clue at a time.
Use words like *red*, *square*, *above*, or *between*.
Give me clues until I guess the secret thing. Then I will be the spy and you can guess.

Community Connection

As you and your child wait in line for, perhaps, a train or a bus, continue the game of I Spy. Your child will be learning the words *under, before, after, above, below, between, top, middle, bottom, left,* and *right.*

💻▫💻 **Visit our Web site. www.parent.mathsurf.com**

Top, Middle, and Bottom

 Notes for home: Your child colored top objects red, middle objects yellow, and bottom objects blue. *Home Activity:* Ask your child to point to and name objects in the top, middle, and bottom drawers of a desk or dresser.

Above and Below

 Notes For Home: Your child used the words *above* and *below* to describe the location of the butterfly and the toy dog in relation to the girl on the bridge. *Home Activity:* Ask your child to use *above* and *below* to tell about objects in relation to his or her head and feet.

Before, After, and Between

Notes for Home: Your child used the words *before*, *after*, and *between* to tell about the picture.
Home Activity: Ask your child to use the words *before*, *after*, and *between* to tell about items as they are removed from a shopping bag.

 Notes for Home: Your child followed specific directions to show the child who is before, after, and between. *Home Activity:* Ask your child to use the words *before, after,* and *between* to tell about events at your evening meal, for example: Mom sat down before I did.

Name _____

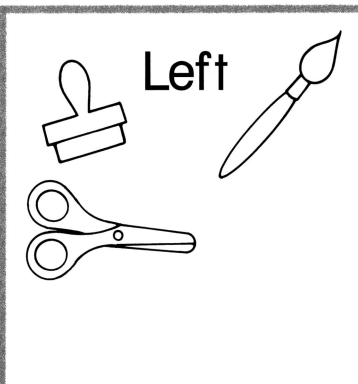

Left

Right

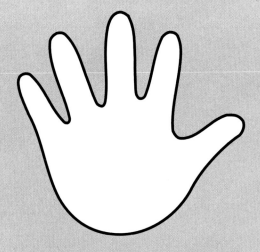

Left

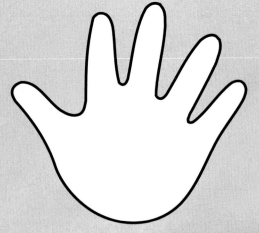

Right

 Notes for Home: Your child circled objects on the left in blue and circled objects on the right in red. *Home Activity:* Ask your child to touch and name objects on the left and objects on the right with his or her left or right hand.

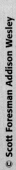

Problem Solving: Making Decisions

Notes for Home: Your child learned about inside and outside. *Home Activity:* Ask your child to use the words *inside* and *outside* to describe objects to go inside the trash can and those that remain outside.

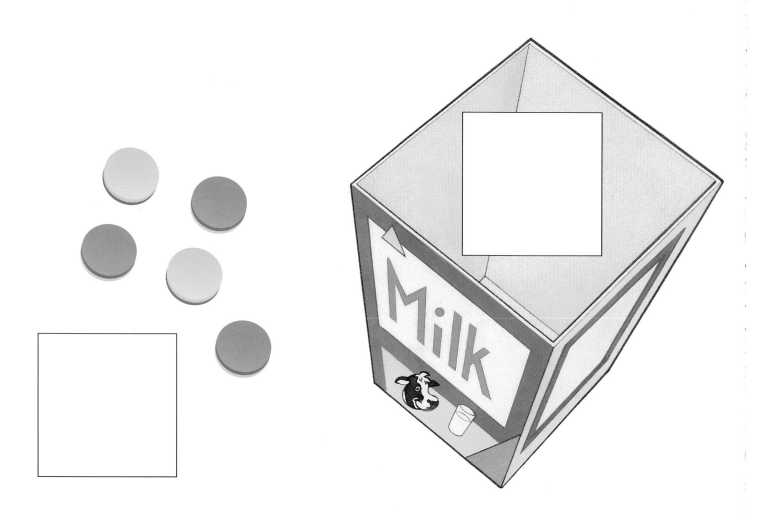

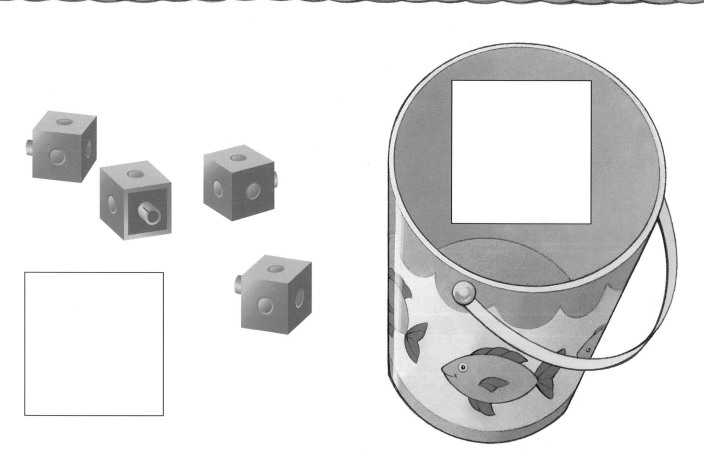

 Notes for Home: Your child made marks to show objects inside and outside each container. *Home Activity:* Ask your child to play one of these games with you and then use the words *inside* and *outside* to tell more about the objects.

Name

 Notes for Home: Your child identified different visual attributes. *Home Activity:* Ask your child to identify attributes of various things such as patent leather shoes, cotton, and a blanket.

 Notes for Home: Your child added to drawings identified by color, size, and shape. *Home Activity:* Ask your child to name objects of a particular color.

Name _____

Same and Different Colors

© Scott Foresman Addison Wesley

Same and Different Shapes and Sizes

 Notes for Home: Your child found and colored shapes that are the same. *Home Activity:* Ask your child to point to two objects in your home and tell if they are the same shape or different shapes.

 Notes for Home: Your child identified buttons that were the same or different sizes.
Home Activity: Ask your child to use the words *same size* and *different size* to compare different objects in or around your home.

Problem Solving: Use Logical Reasoning

Notes for Home: Your child found objects that are out-of-place and told why.
Home Activity: Ask your child to find something out-of-place among his or her belongings. Then ask what makes it out-of-place and where it belongs.

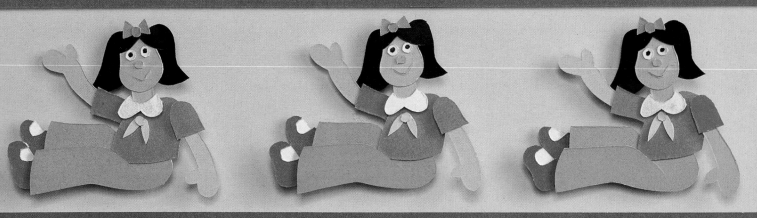

Notes for Home: Have your child circle the object in each row that does not belong and tell why.
Home Activity: Ask your child to tell how the items in each row are the same and how they are different.

Chapter 1 Review/Test

Notes for Home: Your child followed specific directions to show an understanding of position words such as *top, between,* and *inside. Home Activity:* Ask your child to use these and other position words to tell about objects in your home.

Chapter 1 Review/Test

twenty-one 21

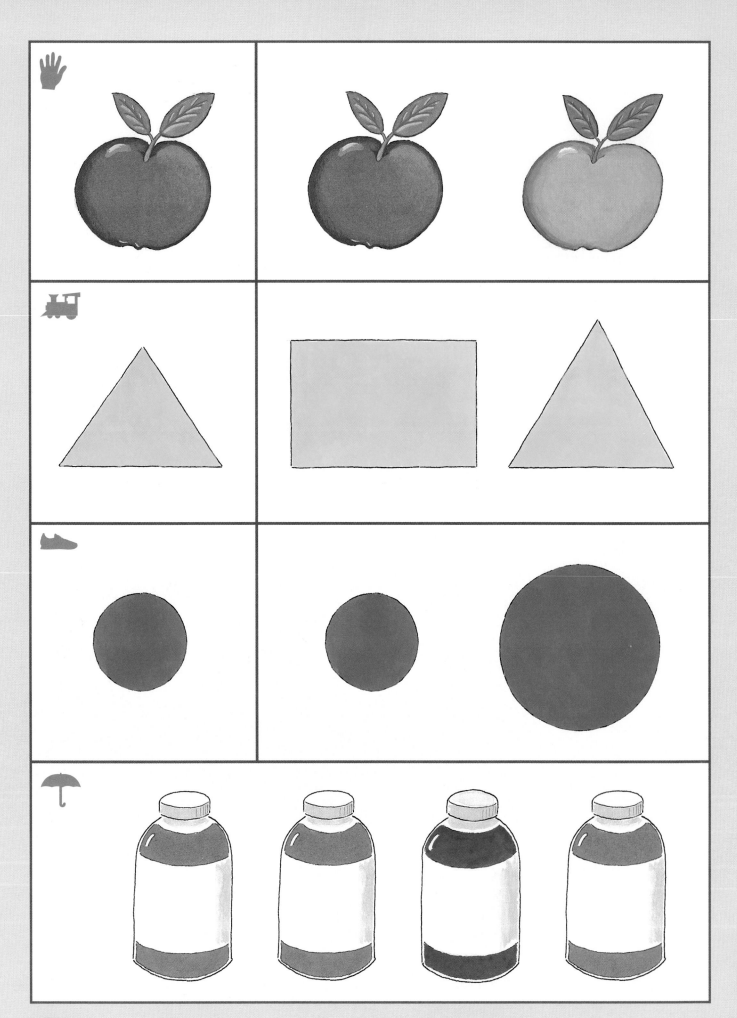

Notes for Home: Your child followed specific directions to circle things that are the same and underline those that are different. *Home Activity:* Ask your child to use the words *same* and *different* to tell about objects in your home.

Play Clay

What You Need

1 bowl
1 spoon
1 1/2 cups flour
1/2 cup salt
1/2 cup water

1/4 cup oil
food coloring

What You Do

1 Mix oil, water, and coloring.

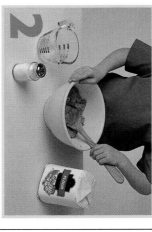

2 Add flour and salt.

3 Make different shapes.

4 Have fun!

Visit our Web site. www.parent.mathsurf.com

Fold down

MathSoup

Scott Foresman - Addison Wesley   My Math Magazine   No. 1

Play with Me

Notes for Home: Your child marked things that are different in the pictures. *Home Activity:* Ask your child to look at a group of objects. Change one of the objects and have your child identify the change.

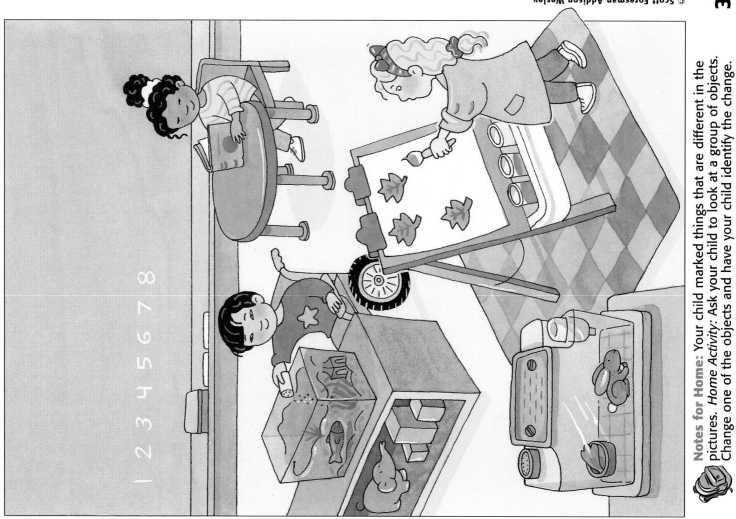

1 2 3 4 5 6 7 8

Math Fun

Second Look

What is different?

Aa Bb Cc Dd Ee Ff Gg Hh

All About Me

Notes for Home: Your child talked about the picture and looked for groups to sort.
Home Activity: Ask your child to point to all the things that are red.

Math at Home

Dear Family,

We will be learning how to sort things.
I can practice sorting by helping
you sort the laundry. Here is
what we can do:

Sort the Laundry
We can sort the laundry in different ways.
We can sort by size.
We can sort by color.
We can sort by type of clothing.
Then I can help you fold my clothes
and put them away.

Community Connection When you are outdoors with your child, choose a shape or color. Look for things that have that shape or color.

💻▫💻 **Visit our Web site.** www.parent.mathsurf.com

© Scott Foresman Addison Wesley

Name _____

Notes for Home: Your child sorted pasta by shape, then drew the shapes. *Home Activity:* Ask your child to sort groceries such as boxes and cans by shape.

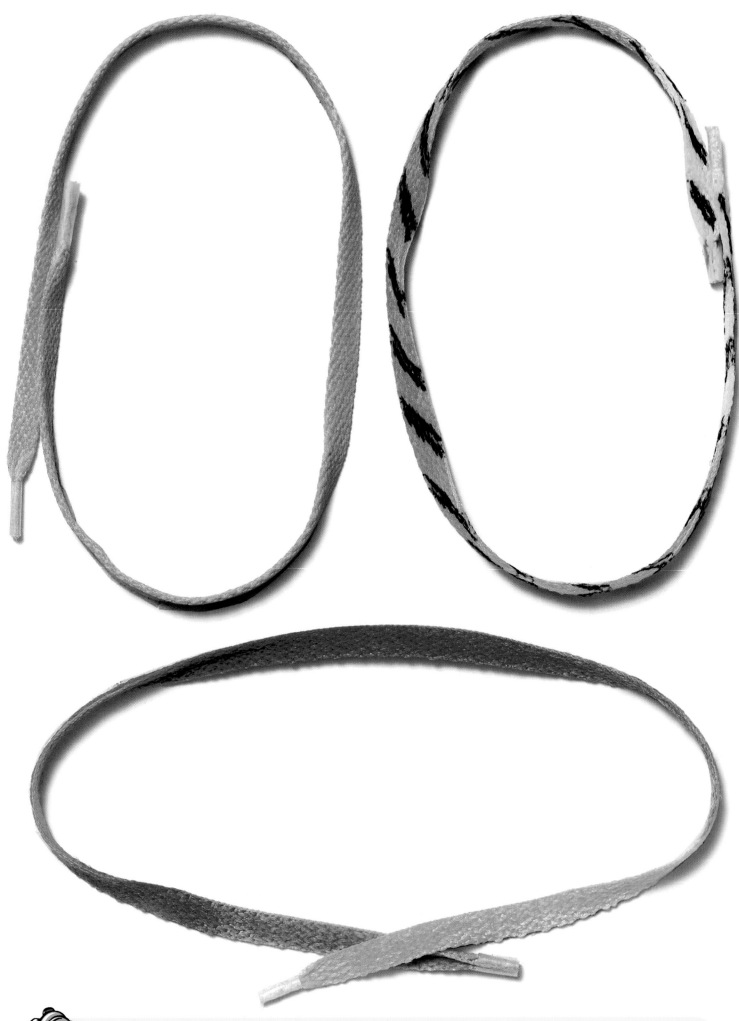

 Notes for Home: Your child sorted Snap Cubes by color, then traced them in the spaces.
Home Activity: Ask your child to sort toys or other objects by color.

Name _____

 Notes for Home: Your child sorted hats two ways by drawing and coloring. *Home Activity:* Ask your child to tell two ways the hats could be sorted.

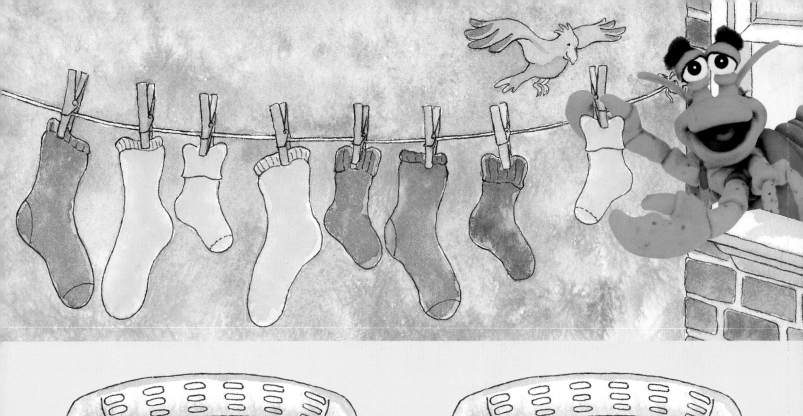

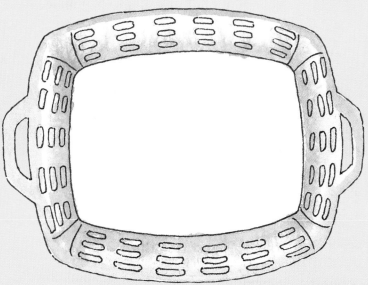
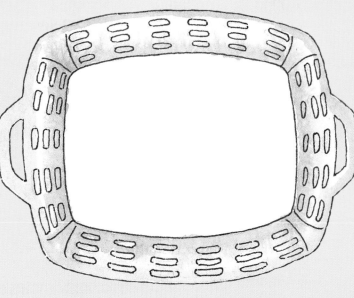

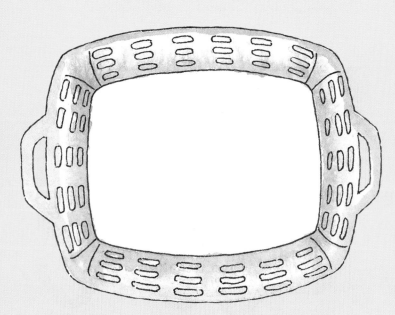
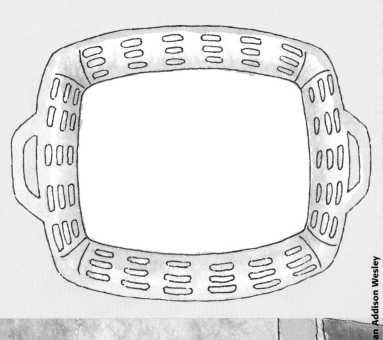

 Notes for Home: Your child drew socks to sort one way and then another way. *Home Activity:* Ask your child to sort socks at home.

As Many As

Notes for Home: Your child matched riders to vehicles to show a one-to-one match.
Home Activity: Ask your child to draw one suitcase for every rider on the page.

More, Fewer

Notes for Home: Your child made Snap Cube trains and decided which train has more cubes.
Home Activity: Ask your child to sort objects at home and tell which group has more or fewer.

More

Fewer

Notes for Home: Your child made and traced cube trains that have more cubes and fewer cubes than the train shown. *Home Activity:* Ask your child to make a stack of plates, then make one stack which is more and one stack which is fewer.

Problem Solving: Use Logical Reasoning

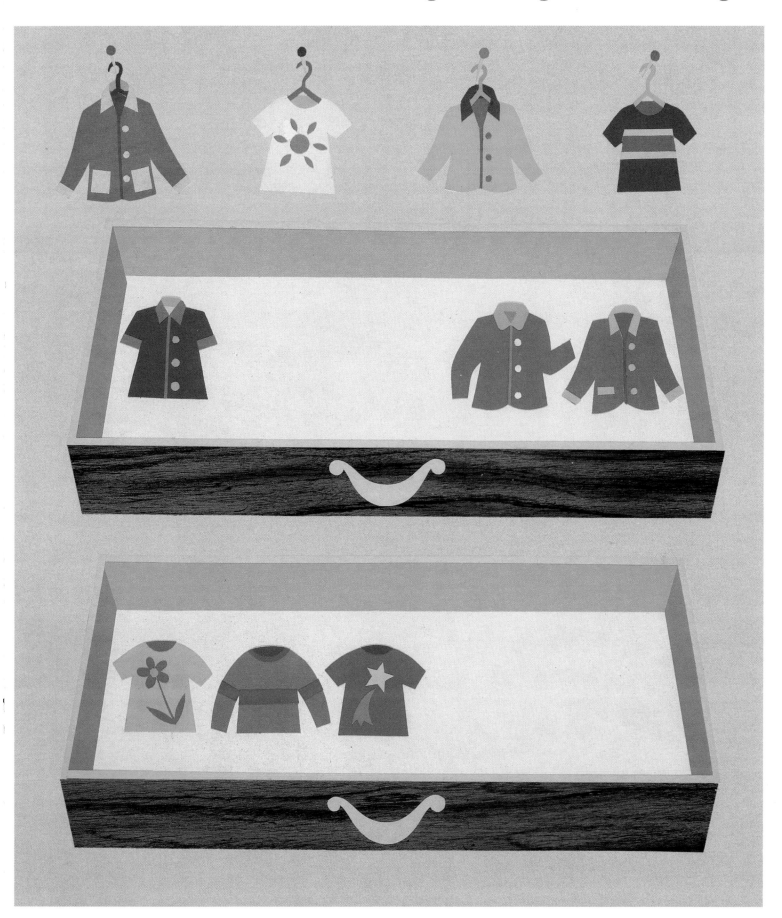

 Notes for Home: Your child drew and colored the shirts that belong in the drawers.
Home Activity: Ask your child to sort some of his or her long and short sleeve shirts into separate groups.

 Notes for Home: Your child colored pictures to show the item that belongs with each group.
Home Activity: Ask your child to sort shoes by size.

Graphs

Are There More Red or Yellow?

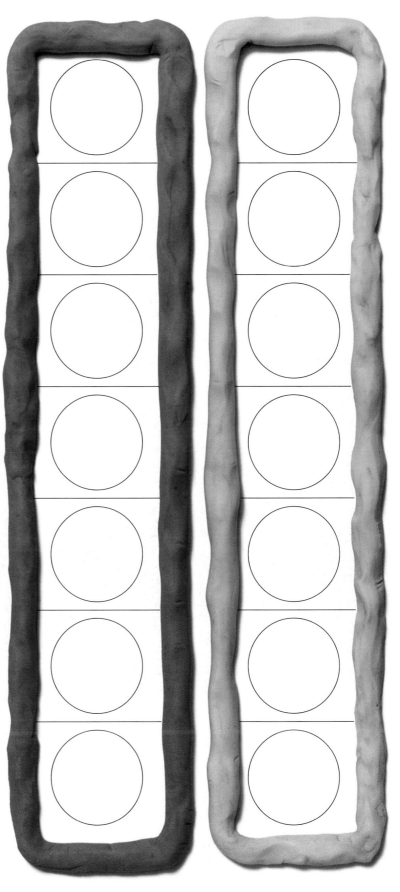

Notes for Home: Your child tossed counters and made a graph to show red or yellow, then drew a blue line under the column with more counters. *Home Activity:* Ask your child to toss 8 pennies and make a graph showing heads or tails. Talk about whether the graph shows more heads or tails.

Are There More White or Brown Beans?

Picture Graphs

Which Toy Do You Like Better?

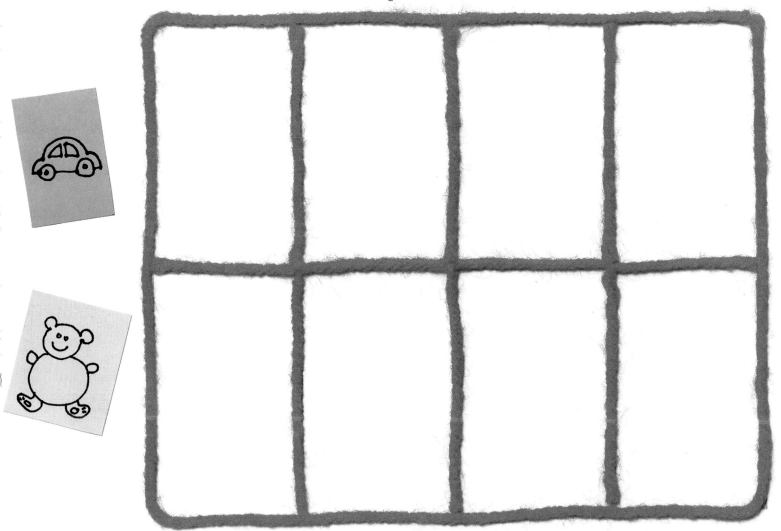

 Notes for Home: Your child surveyed a group to find out whether wheel toys or stuffed animals were the favorite. *Home Activity:* Ask your child to find out if family members favor indoor or outdoor games.

Which Pet Would You Rather Have?

Notes for Home: Have your child label each row by drawing a picture of a different type of pet, then survey family about favorite pets. Your child can then draw pictures to show the choices.
Home Activity: Ask your child to take a favorite food survey and draw the results on a graph.

Name

Problem Solving: Use Data from a Graph

Favorite Outdoor Games

Favorite Indoor Games

 Notes for Home: Your child used a picture graph to decide which activity is the favorite.
Home Activity: Ask your child to find out what family activity is the favorite.

Name _____

Chapter 2 Review/Test

 Notes for Home: Your child was assessed on math ideas in Chapter 2. He or she drew pictures to sort and compare items. *Home Activity:* Ask your child to sort toys by size and then color.

Things in the Toy Box

 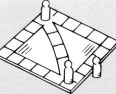 

Kitchen Helper

Where do these go?
Draw them in their place.

FROZEN YOGURT

SPAGHETTI

CRACKERS

SOAP

SOUP

Fold down

MathSurf

Scott Foresman - Addison Wesley   My Math Magazine   No. 2

Come See My Room!

My Crazy Room

What does not belong?

Math Fun

Notes for Home: Your child circled things in the picture that do not belong. *Home Activity:* Ask your child to tell you why each circled thing does not belong.

Explore Patterns

Looking for Changes

Notes for Home: Your child talked about things that changed from panel to panel in the quilt. *Home Activity:* Look at wallpaper or a decorative border. Help your child identify something that appears over and over, and talk about what changes and what stays the same.

Math at Home

Dear Family,
We will be learning that a pattern is created when something changes and the change repeats over and over. We will explore where to find patterns and how to recognize them. Here is something you and I can do together:

Play "Follow the Leader."
You be the leader.
Decide on a movement like HOP.
Then change the movement to CLAP.
Repeat the HOP, CLAP over and over.
I will figure out the repeating part and do it for you. Then we can do it together.
We can do more of these on another day.

Community Connection

When you visit the park or some other recreational area with your child, you could play a "Follow the Leader" game taking turns establishing and following a variety of walking patterns.

Visit our Web site. www.parent.mathsurf.com

Find a Pattern

 Notes for Home: Your child recorded color patterns by following those in the pictures.
Home Activity: Ask your child to find patterns in wallpaper, clothing, blankets, or borders on dishes.

 Notes for Home: Your child found different patterns and colored the boxes to match one.
Home Activity: Make a two-color pattern by arranging some kitchen objects, and ask your child to identify it.

50   fifty

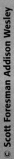

Copy and Extend Patterns

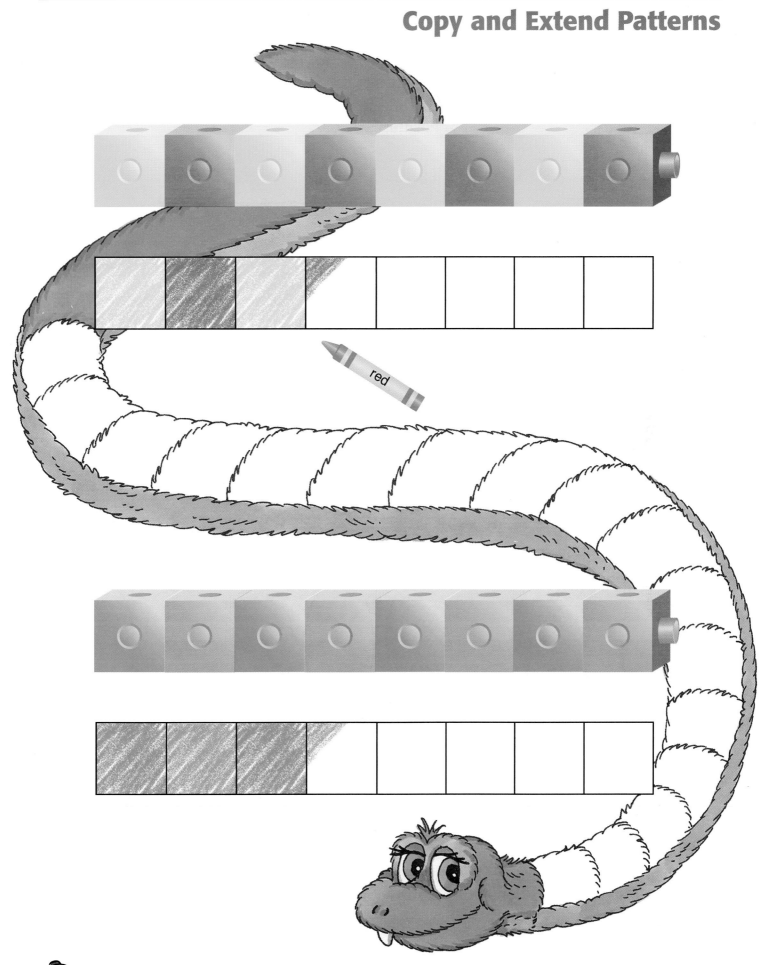

red

Notes for Home: Your child copied two-color patterns. *Home Activity:* Use crayons to draw a pattern of circles in two colors. Ask your child to copy your pattern.

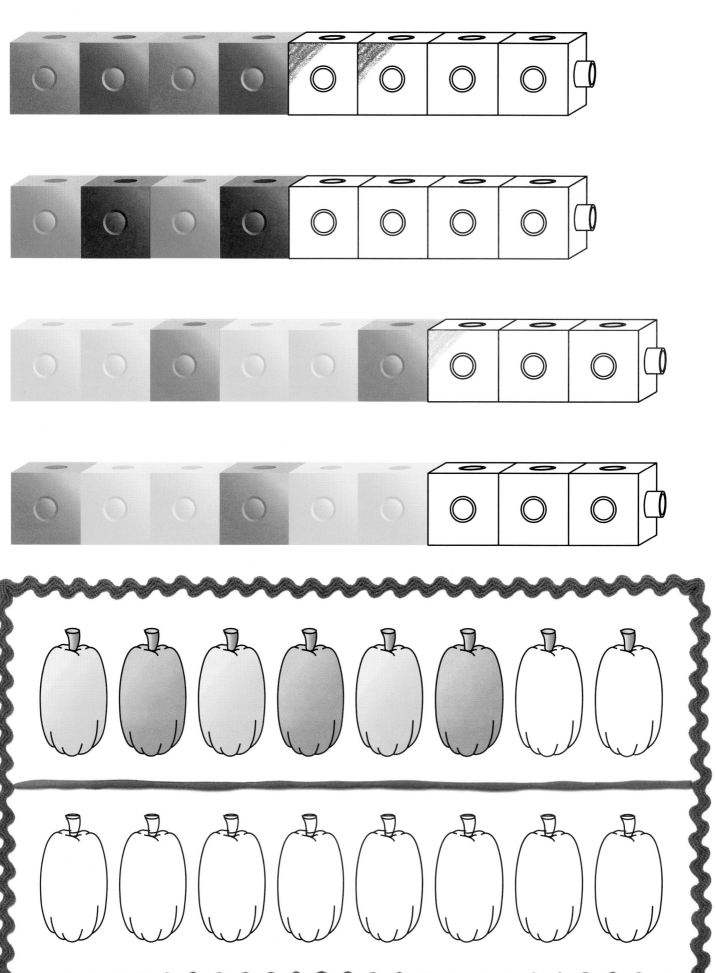

Notes for Home: Your child colored to continue the patterns. *Home Activity:* Use pennies and nickels to make a pattern. Ask your child to tell what comes next.

Make Patterns

 Notes for Home: Your child chose colors and created his or her own patterns.
Home Activity: Give your child sets of objects such as pens, pencils, and crayons, and let him or her show you how to make a pattern.

Name _____

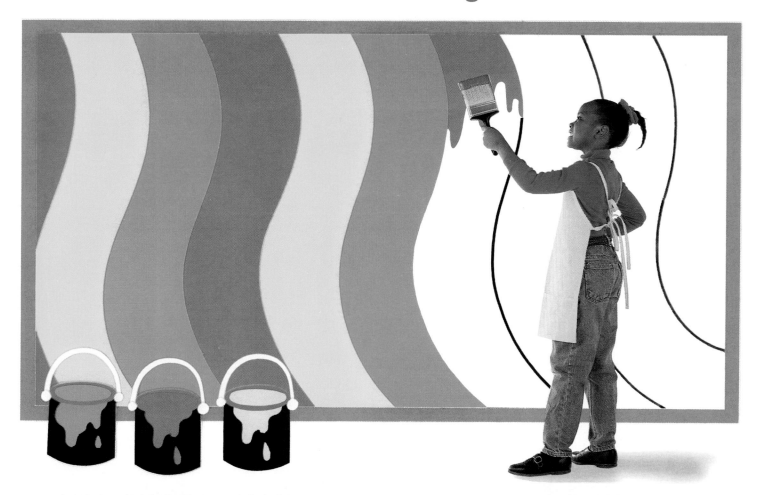

 Notes for Home: Your child solved problems by finding patterns and completing them.
Home Activity: Begin setting your dinner table. Ask your child to finish by following your pattern.

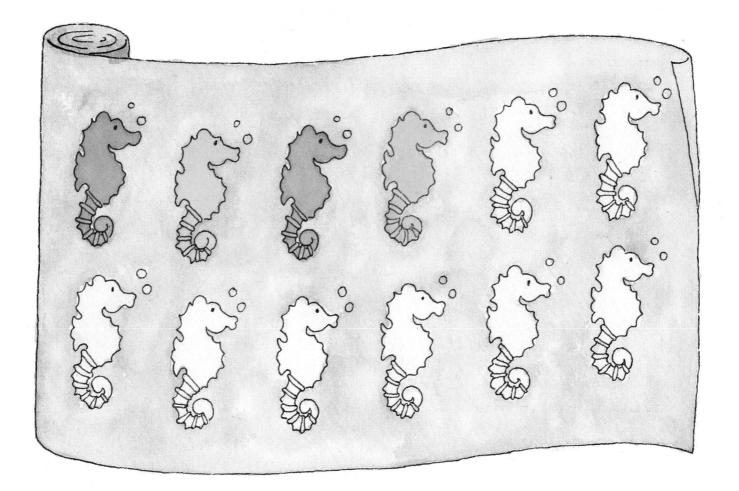

 Notes for Home: Your child completed the wallpaper patterns on this page. *Home Activity:* Ask your child to use shapes cut from colored paper to make a two-color pattern.

Name _____

Notes for Home: Your child found patterns that are alike. *Home Activity:* Ask your child to use different items to make patterns that are alike, for example: nickel, dime, nickel, dime and fork, spoon, fork, spoon.

Name

Show Patterns in Different Ways

Notes for Home: Your child identified a pattern shown 3 ways, then showed it a fourth way.
Home Activity: Model a pattern in movement or sound, for example: clap, snap, clap, snap.
Help your child find that same pattern in something visual, perhaps 2 colors or 2 shapes.

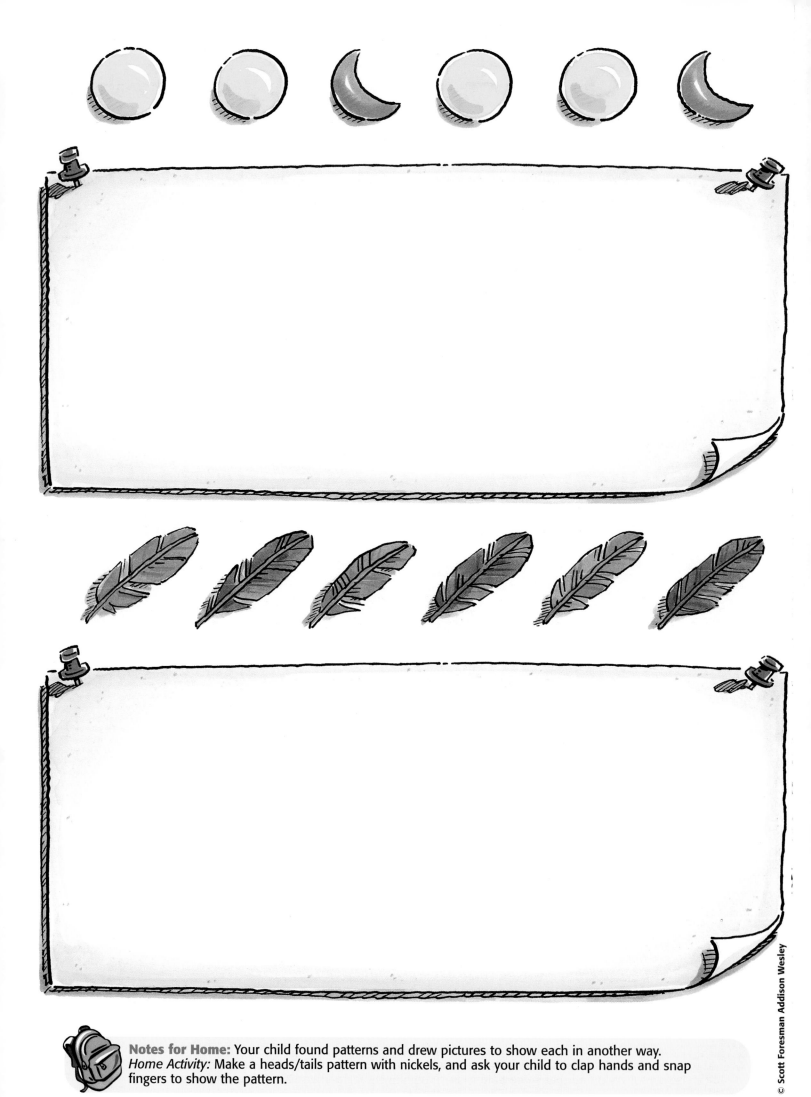

Name

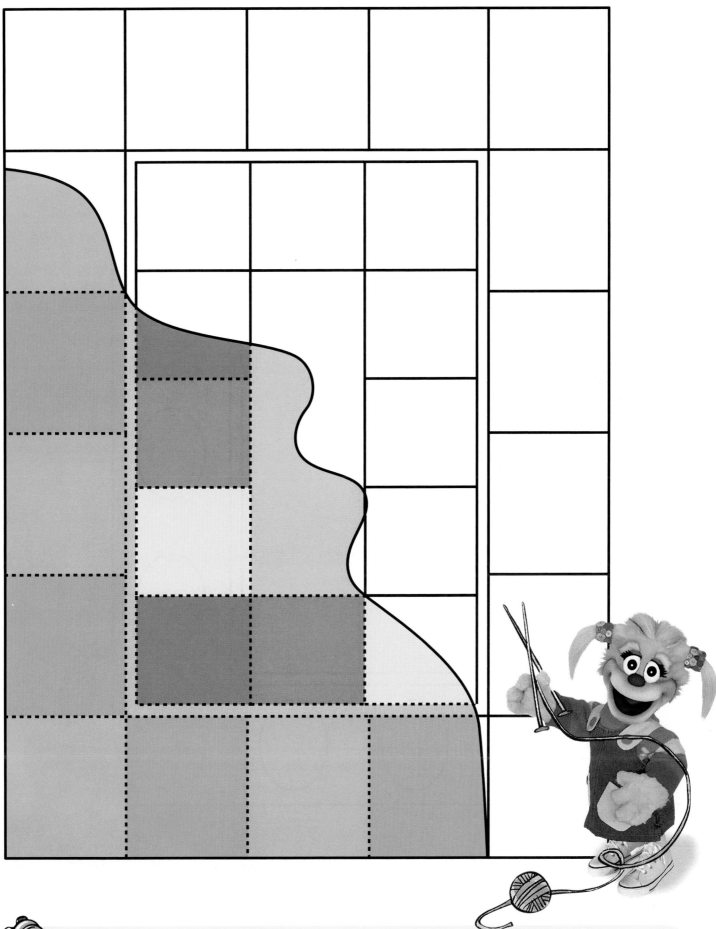

Notes for Home: Your child predicted what elements of the patterns were missing and finished coloring. *Home Activity:* Ask your child to talk about patterns you find at home, such as borders on handkerchiefs, wallpaper, and so on.

Notes for Home: Your child predicted what elements of the patterns were missing and finished coloring. *Home Activity:* Ask your child to talk about various patterns on clothing.

62 sixty-two

Name _____

Chapter 3 Review/Test

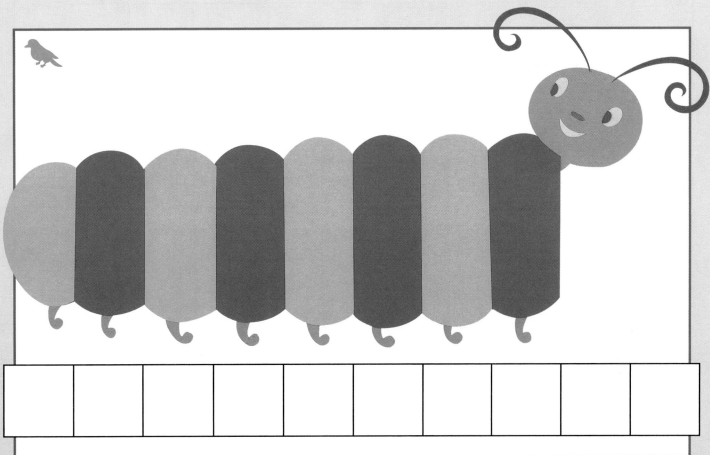

 Notes for Home: In the first row your child copied a pattern and continued it. In the second row, he or she found two patterns that are the same and one that is different. *Home Activity:* Ask your child to tell you about a pattern in your home.

Notes for Home: Your child completed the pattern on each rug. *Home Activity:* Have your child continue a pattern that you begin, such as red, yellow, red, yellow, and so on.

Pasta Patterns

What You Need

Scissors

3 Kinds of Pasta

String

What You Do

3

4

1

2

Fold down

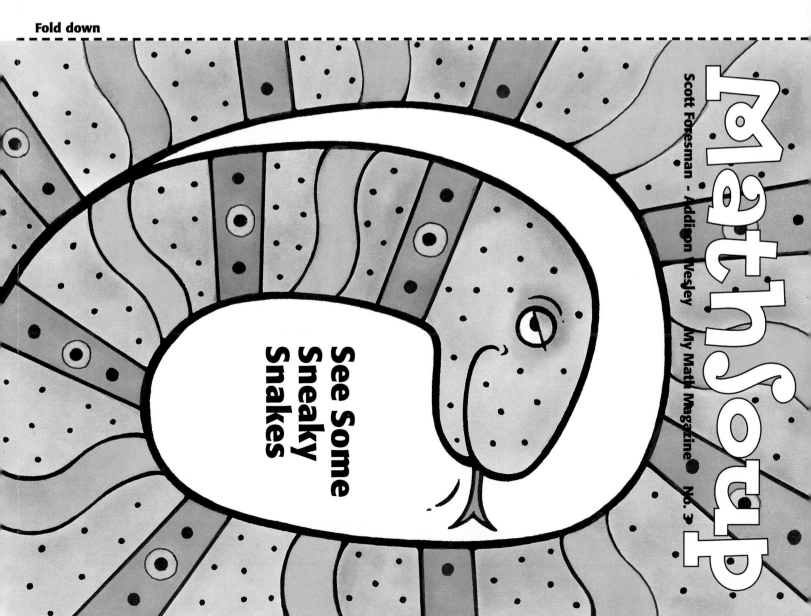

See Some Sneaky Snakes

Scott Foresman · Addison Wesley

My Math Magazine · No. 3

MathSurf

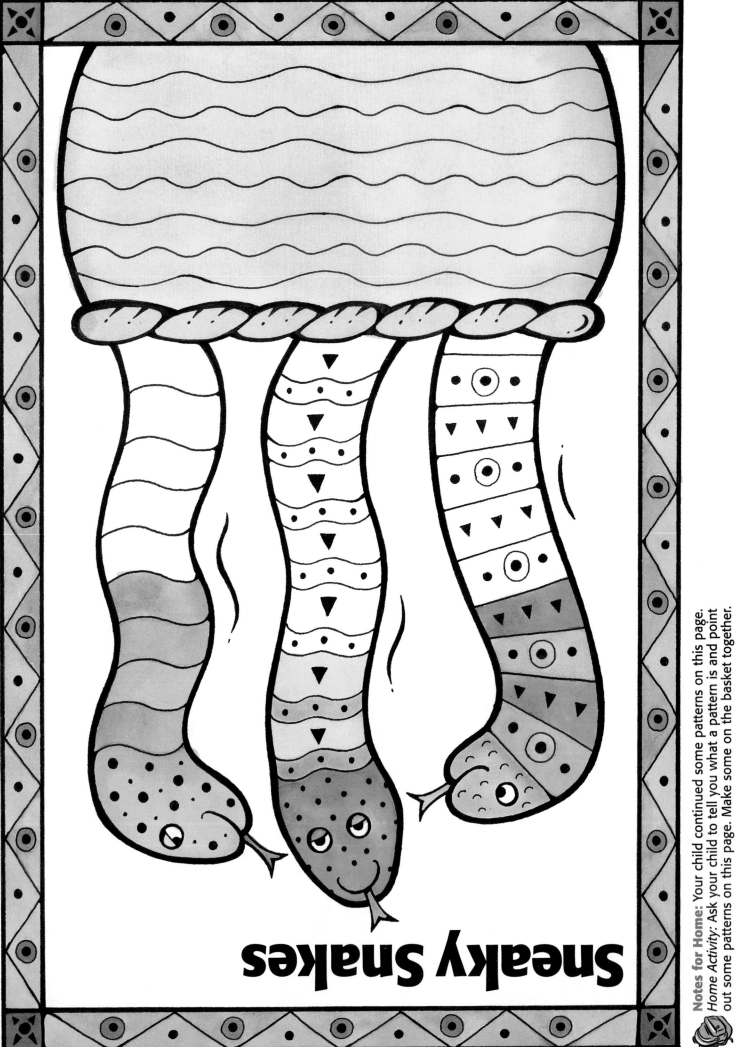

Sneaky Snakes

Notes for Home: Your child continued some patterns on this page.
Home Activity: Ask your child to tell you what a pattern is and point
out some patterns on this page. Make some on the basket together.

Math Fun

2

Families and Friends

Notes for Home: Your child talked about the groups of people and objects in the picture. *Home Activity:* Ask your child to tell you about one of the groups in the picture.

Math at Home

Dear Family,
We will be learning how to count and write numbers to 5. I can practice counting by helping you set the table. Here is what we can do.

Set the Table
Decide how many places to set.
Count the number of forks we need.
Count the number of spoons we need.
Count the number of napkins we need.
Count the number of plates we need.
Set the table together.

Community Connection

When you and your child walk or drive through your neighborhood, point out groups of 1 to 5 things, for example: I see 5 trees across the street. I see 2 dogs playing in that yard. I see 1 stop sign at the corner.

💻▫💻 **Visit our Web site.** www.parent.mathsurf.com

Name

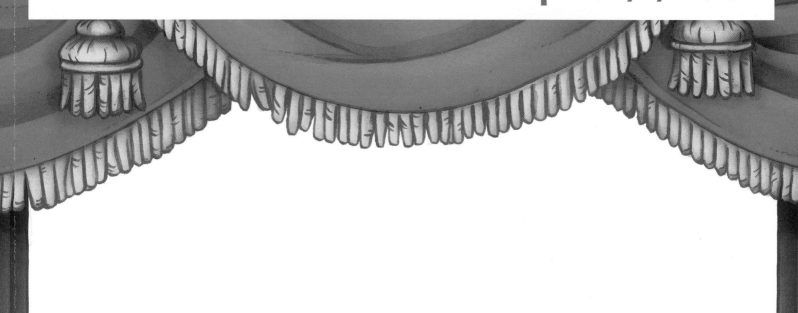

Notes for Home: Your child made a group of 1, 2, or 3 puppets. *Home Activity:* Ask your child to tell you a story about the puppets.

1

2

3

Notes for Home: Your child read the number in each box and drew pictures to show how many.
Home Activity: Ask your child to draw pictures for you that show 1, 2, and 3.

70   seventy

Name _____

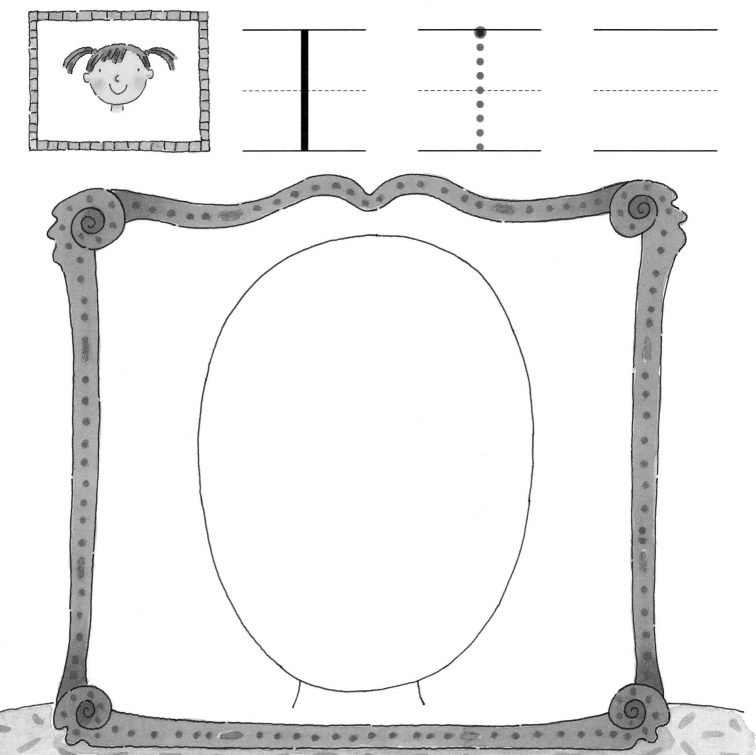

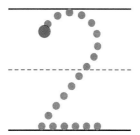

 Notes for Home: Your child made a friendly face to show groups of 1 and 2. *Home Activity:* Ask your child to draw a friendly face for you and tell how many eyes, ears, noses, and mouths it has.

1

2

Name _____

3   ⦿⦿⦿   _____

___   seventy-three

Notes for Home: Your child practiced writing 3, then drew pictures of groups of 3.
Home Activity: Ask your child to use small objects such as pennies to show you a group of 3 things.

1 2 3

1

2

3

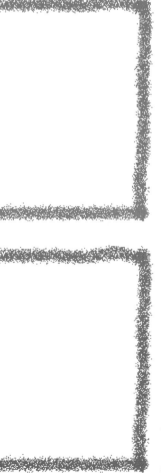

© Scott Foresman Addison Wesley

Notes for Home: Have your child practice writing 1, 2, and 3, then draw pictures to show you groups of 1, 2, and 3. *Home Activity:* Ask your child to help you write the numbers 1, 2, and 3 to label things around your house.

74 seventy-four

Name _____

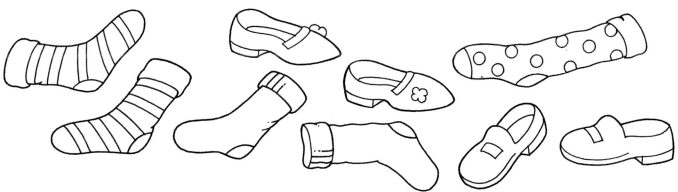

 Notes for Home: Your child looked for groups of 4 and 5 objects in the picture, then marked 4 things red and 5 things blue. *Home Activity:* Ask your child to show you groups of 4 and 5 objects in your home.

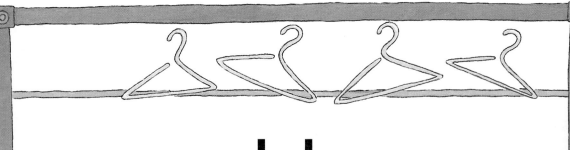

4

5

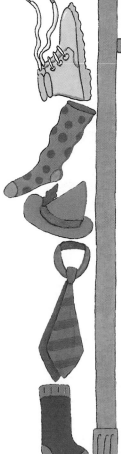

 Notes for Home: Your child drew a group of 4 items and a group of 5 items in a closet.
Home Activity: Ask your child to find a group of 4 or 5 things in a closet at home.

Name _____

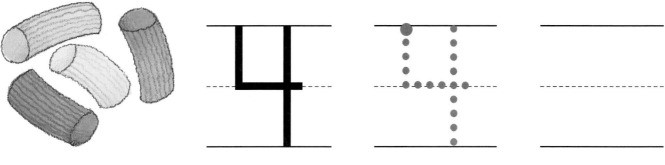

Count and Write 4

4   ┊┊┊   seventy-seven

Notes for Home: Your child made and recorded different groups of 4 objects. *Home Activity:* Ask your child to make a group of 4 things on a table at home.

Notes for Home: Your child arranged torn paper to make groups of 4, then practiced writing 4.
Home Activity: Ask your child to show you how to write 4.

Name _____

5   5   _____

_____   _____

Notes for Home: Your child drew pictures of groups of 5 objects, then wrote the number 5.
Home Activity: Ask your child to show you a group of 5 objects, such as 5 pennies.

5

3

2

5

© Scott Foresman Addison Wesley

Notes for Home: Your child wrote numbers or drew pictures to show groups of 1 to 5 puppets.
Home Activity: Ask your child to draw a picture for you that shows a group of 5.

Explore and Write 0

Notes for Home: Your child talked about empty plates to learn what zero means.
Home Activity: Ask your child to show you a plate on which there are 2 things and a plate on which there is nothing or 0 things.

Chapter 4 Lesson 7

eighty-one 81

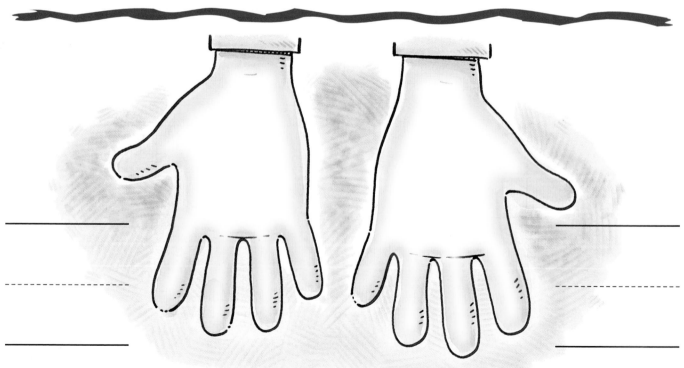

 Notes for Home: Your child played a guessing game and drew pictures to show what happened. *Home Activity:* Hold several pennies in one hand and no pennies in the other hand. Show your child both hands and ask which hand has no pennies or 0.

82   eighty-two

Problem Solving: Use Objects

 Notes for Home: Your child used counters to decide if there is a red balloon for each child.
Home Activity: Set out seven pennies. Ask your child to use counters to decide if there is a penny for
each of these four children.

 Notes for Home: Your child drew a picture of a family or group of friends, then showed a plate for each person. *Home Activity:* Ask your child to tell you a story about a picnic.

Name

Notes for Home: Your child identified and talked about groups of 1, 2, 3, 4, and 5 in the picture. He or she colored the caps of each group a different color. *Home Activity:* Ask your child to arrange groups of pennies or toothpicks in order from 1 to 5.

Notes for Home: Your child colored cubes to show a sequence of groups from 1 to 5, then drew ears of corn to show the missing numbers. *Home Activity:* Ask your child to show you groups of 1 to 5 toys in sequence.

Order Numbers to 5

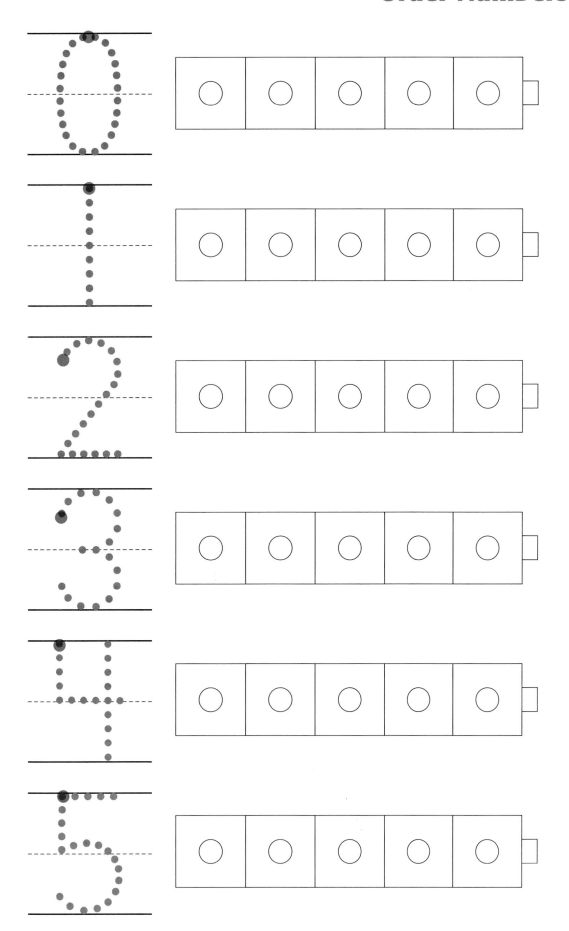

Notes for Home: Your child colored and then wrote numbers to show 0 to 5 in order.
Home Activity: Ask your child to count 5 steps aloud, starting from 0.

Notes for Home: Your child drew groups to show 0–5 in order, then wrote numbers.
Home Activity: Ask your child to hold up 0 through 5 fingers in order.

Compare Numbers to 5

 Notes for Home: Your child compared the numbers in groups of objects. *Home Activity:* Ask your child to tell how he or she knows that there were more forks than spoons before drawing.

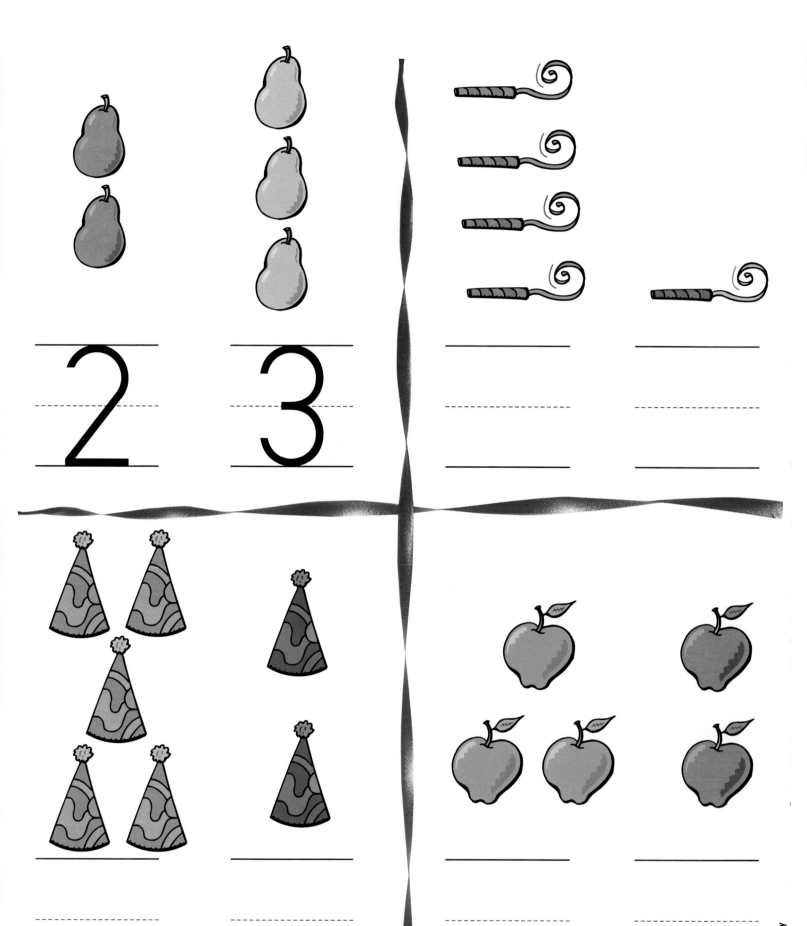

2   3

Notes for Home: Your child compared groups, wrote numbers, and circled groups with more and
fewer. *Home Activity:* Ask your child to tell you how he or she knows that a group of 5 people is more
than a group of 3 people.

90   ninety

Problem Solving: Draw a Picture

Notes for Home: Your child listened to a story and drew pictures to help solve a problem.
Home Activity: Ask your child to draw a picture to show how many plates are needed if everyone in your family eats dinner together.

Chapter 4 Lesson 12   ninety-one **91**

Chapter 4 Review/Test

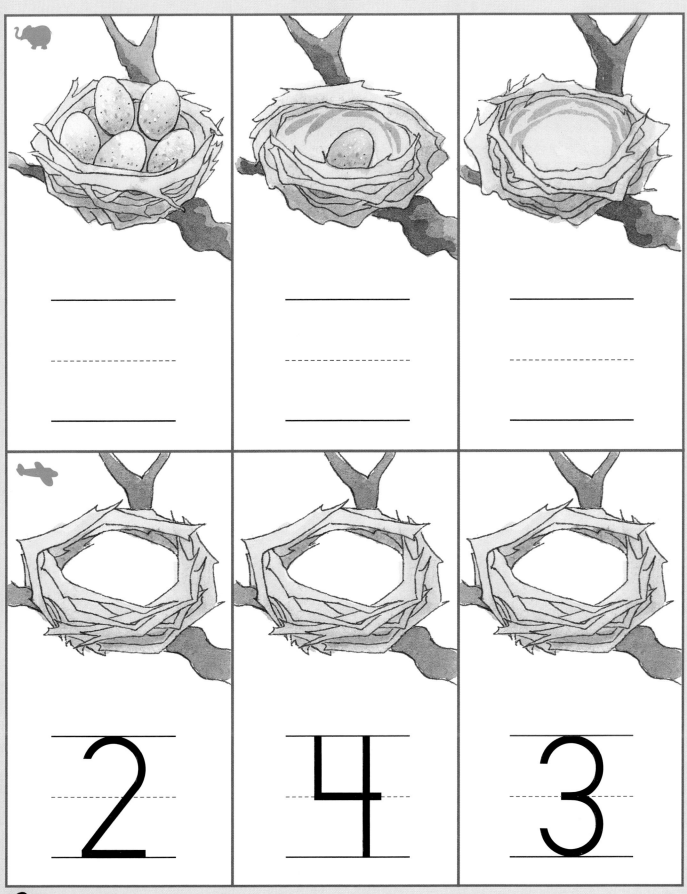

Notes for Home: Your child was assessed on the math ideas in Chapter 4. In the top row, he or she wrote numbers to match the numbers of eggs. In the bottom row, he or she drew pictures to match the numbers. *Home Activity:* Ask your child to point to the nest showing 5 eggs.

More

Fewer

| 0 | 1 | | 3 | | 5 |

Notes for Home: Your child was assessed on the math ideas in Chapter 4. He or she drew more or fewer objects and put numbers 0 to 5 in order. *Home Activity:* Ask your child to count from 0 to 5, as he or she points to each number.

Funny Face

Make a sandwich for someone you love.

What You Need

1 Plastic Knife

1 Rice Cake

3 Banana Slices

1 Jar of Peanut Butter

5 Raisins

What You do

1

2

3

4

Fold down

Make a Funny Face

MathSurf

Scott Foresman - Addison Wesley

My Math Magazine   No. 4

Find It!

Find the numbers.
Ring the objects.

1
2
3
4
5

Notes for Home: Your child found and circled these objects in the picture: 1 toy car, 2 suitcases, 3 light bulbs, 4 birds, 5 stars. *Home Activity:* Ask your child to point out any numbers in the picture too.

Good Night

Notes for Home: Your child talked about groups of things in the picture. *Home Activity:* Ask your child to show you a group of 9 things in your yard or elsewhere outside your home.

Dear Family,

We will be learning how to count and write numbers from 6 to 10. I can practice counting by helping make snack bags.

Here is what we can do.

Make Snack Bags

We will need 5 small plastic bags. We will need small snack foods such as raisins, pretzels, or peanuts. Tell me how many snacks to put in each bag. I will count the snacks and put them into the bag. We can save the bags to use when I want a snack.

Community Connection

When you are out in your neighborhood, invite your child to look for the numbers 6, 7, 8, 9, or 10 in your surroundings. Look for the numbers on house addresses, license plates, street signs, and so on.

Visit our Web site. www.parent.mathsurf.com

Name _____

6

7

8

 Notes for Home: Your child read the number in each box and arranged counters to show how many.
Home Activity: Ask your child to show you a group of 6, 7, or 8 objects in your home.

6

7

8

Notes for Home: Your child drew 5 counters in each box and then drew more to show 6, 7, or 8.
Home Activity: Ask your child to draw and count groups of 7 objects.

100   one hundred

Name _____

6   6   ___

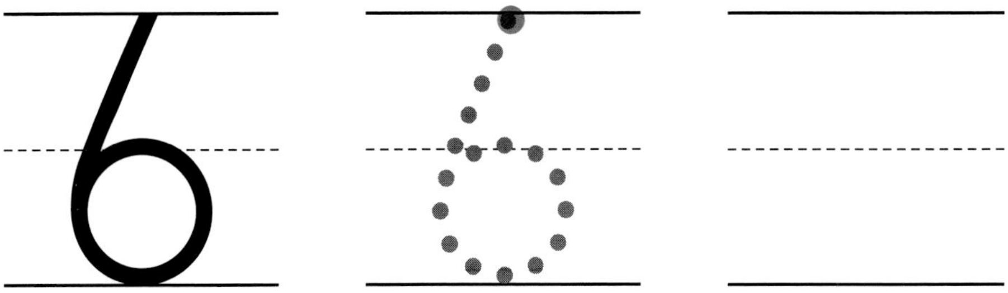

Notes for Home: Your child wrote 6 and recorded arrangements of 6 counters.
Home Activity: Ask your child to show you different combinations of 6 fingers.

6

Notes for Home: Your child practiced writing 6, then drew pictures of groups of 6.
Home Activity: Ask your child to show you a group of 6 things and write the number 6
to label the group.

Count and Write 7

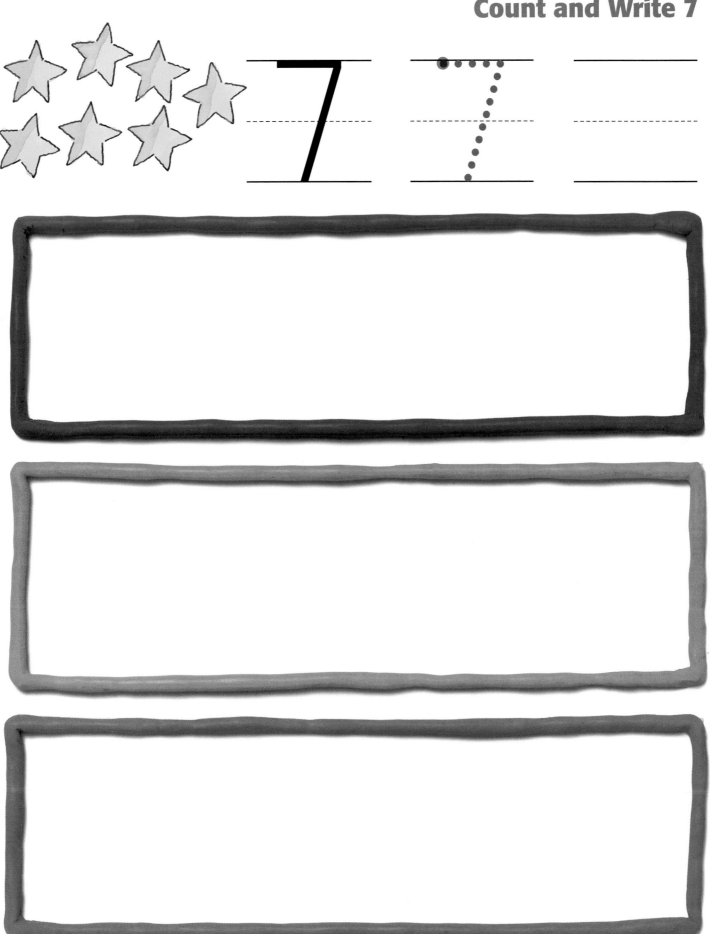

 Notes for Home: Your child wrote 7 and made groups of 7 objects. *Home Activity:* Ask your child to make a group of 7 pennies or other small objects.

7   7

6

5

4

Notes for Home: Help your child write 7, 6, 5, and 4 and then draw pictures to represent those numbers. *Home Activity:* Ask your child to find and count a group of 7 things at home.

Count and Write 8

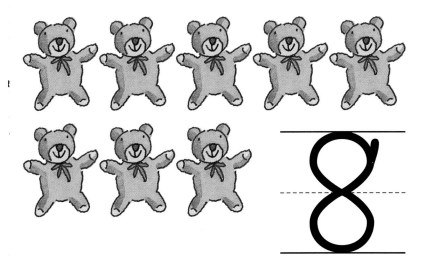

8

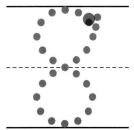

 Notes for Home: Your child practiced writing 8, then made groups of 8 objects.
Home Activity: Ask your child to count the legs on two chairs or two tables and write how many.

Chapter 5 Lesson 4   one hundred five   105

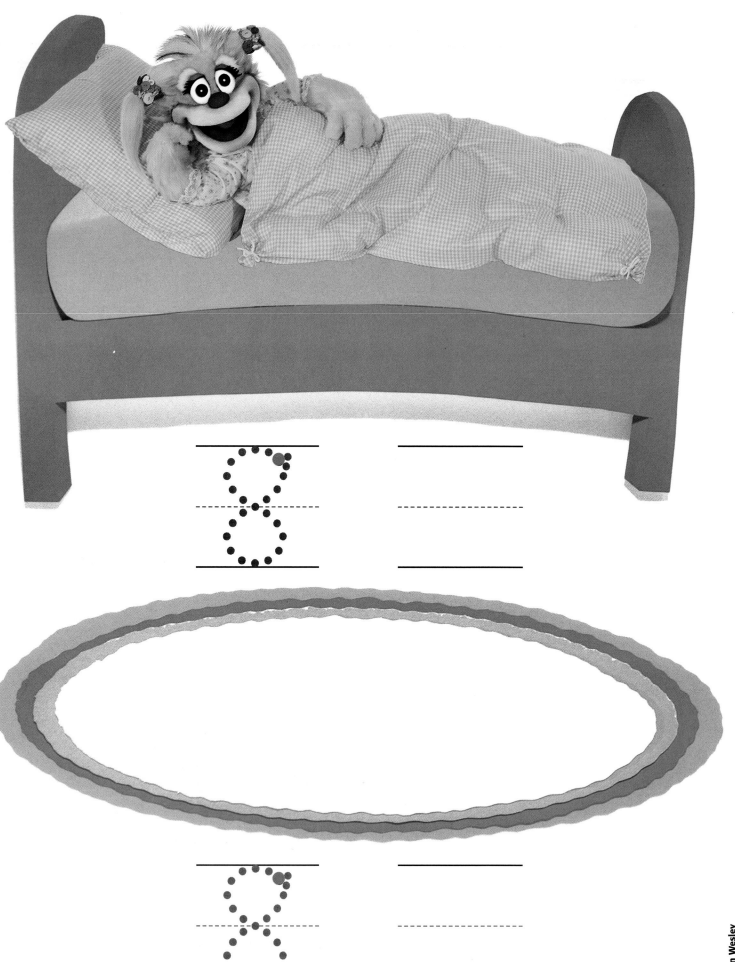

 Notes for Home: Your child made arrangements of 8 objects, then practiced number writing.
Home Activity: Ask your child to find and label a group of 8 objects at home.

Explore 9 and 10

Notes for Home: Your child looked for groups of 9 and 10 in the picture, then colored a leaf for each cricket and a stump for each raccoon. *Home Activity:* Ask your child to take 9 giant steps while walking to bed.

Chapter 5 Lesson 5 one hundred seven **107**

9

10

© Scott Foresman Addison Wesley

Notes for Home: Your child made arrangements of 9 and 10 counters. *Home Activity:* Ask your child to make and count a group of 9 coins and a group of 10 coins.

Name _____

 9 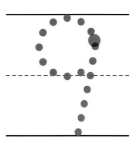 _____

 Notes for Home: Your child practiced writing 9 and then drew pictures or pasted objects to show groups of 9 stars. *Home Activity:* Ask your child to count 9 objects and write the number 9.

9

Notes for Home: Your child wrote numbers and drew pictures to show things in the night sky.
Home Activity: Ask your child to show 9 fingers.

110   one hundred ten

Name _____

 Notes for Home: Your child practiced writing 10 and then drew 10 windows in the building.
Home Activity: Ask your child to count the fingers on your hands and write the number.

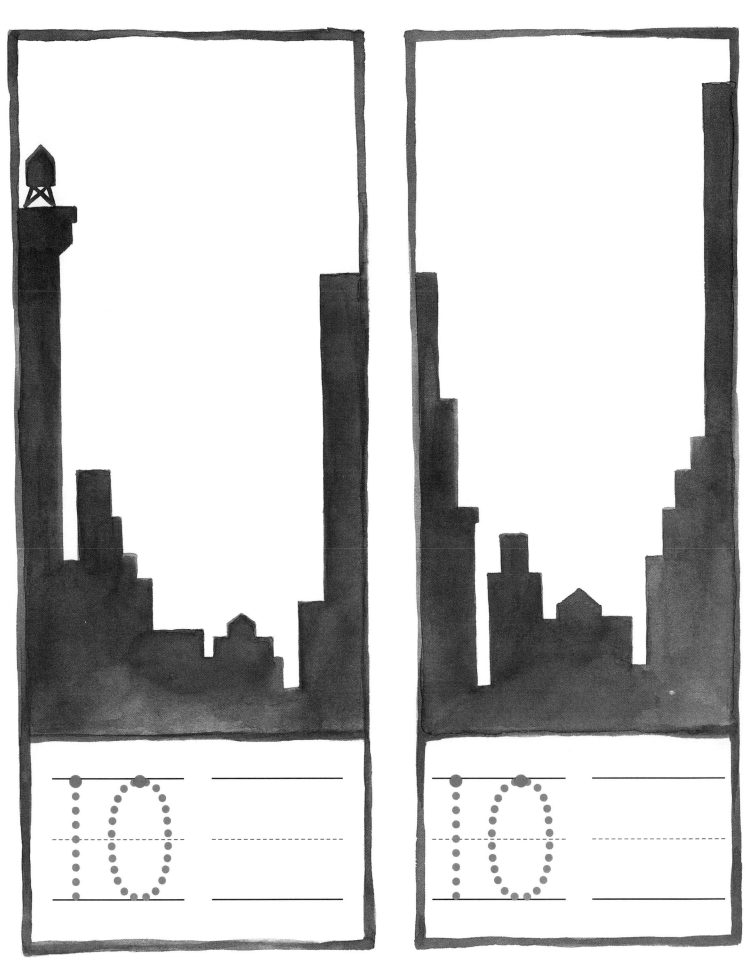

Notes for Home: Your child made arrangements of 10 counters, then practiced writing 10.
Home Activity: Ask your child to show you how to write the number 10.

Problem Solving: Use Data from a Picture

 Notes for Home: Your child looked at the top picture to find groups containing 1 more than the group shown in each row, drew them, and wrote how many. *Home Activity:* Point out a group of objects in your home, and ask your child to find a group that has 1 more.

Name _____

<table>
<tr><td></td><td></td><td></td><td></td><td></td><td></td><td></td><td></td><td></td><td></td></tr>
</table>

Notes for Home: Your child colored cube trains to show a sequence of groups from 1 to 10.
Home Activity: Ask your child to use beans or coins to show a sequence of groups from 1 to 10.

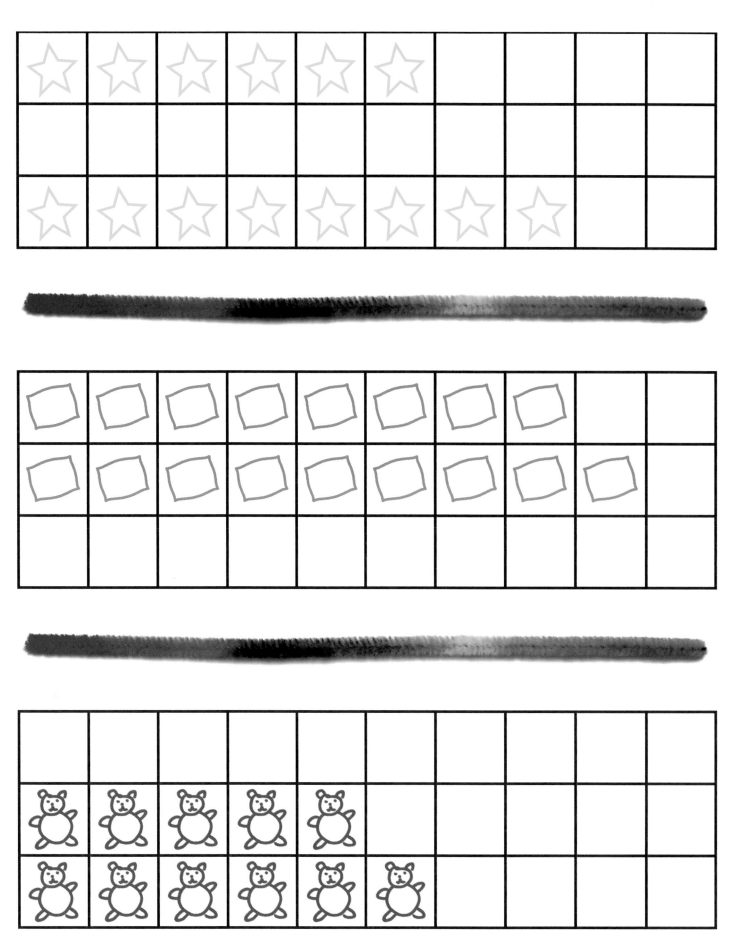

Notes for Home: Your child drew a missing group of objects in each sequence. *Home Activity:* Ask your child to show you 3 groups of toys in sequence.

116   one hundred sixteen

Name _____

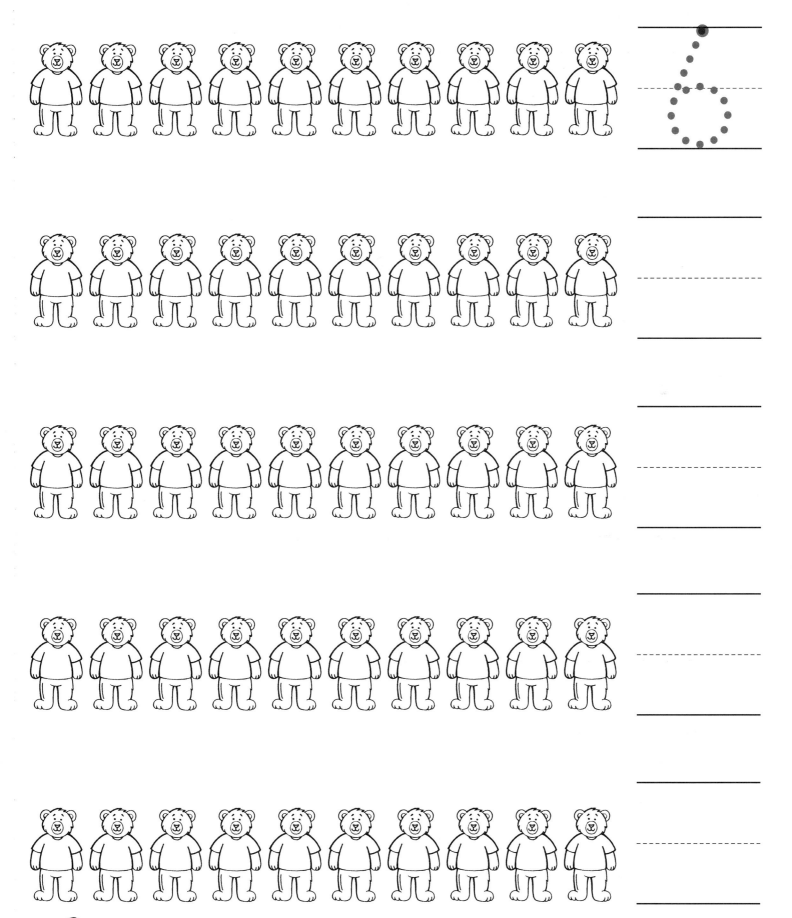

Notes for Home: Your child colored the bears to show the order from 6 to 10 and wrote the numbers to match. *Home Activity:* Ask your child to count 1 to 10 steps as you walk together.

 Notes for Home: Your child wrote the missing numbers, in each row. *Home Activity:* Ask your child what number comes before and after a given number between 1 and 10.

Compare Numbers to 5 and 10

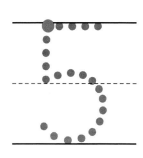

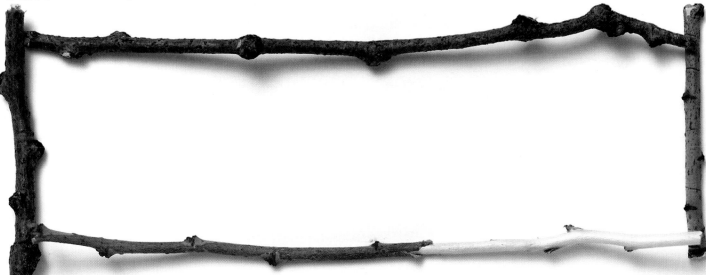

 Notes for Home: Your child put a blue sky in the box with fewer than 5, green grass in the boxes with more than 5, a yellow sun in the box with a group equal to 5, and drew a group of 5. *Home Activity*: Ask your child to show you a group of more than 5 household objects.

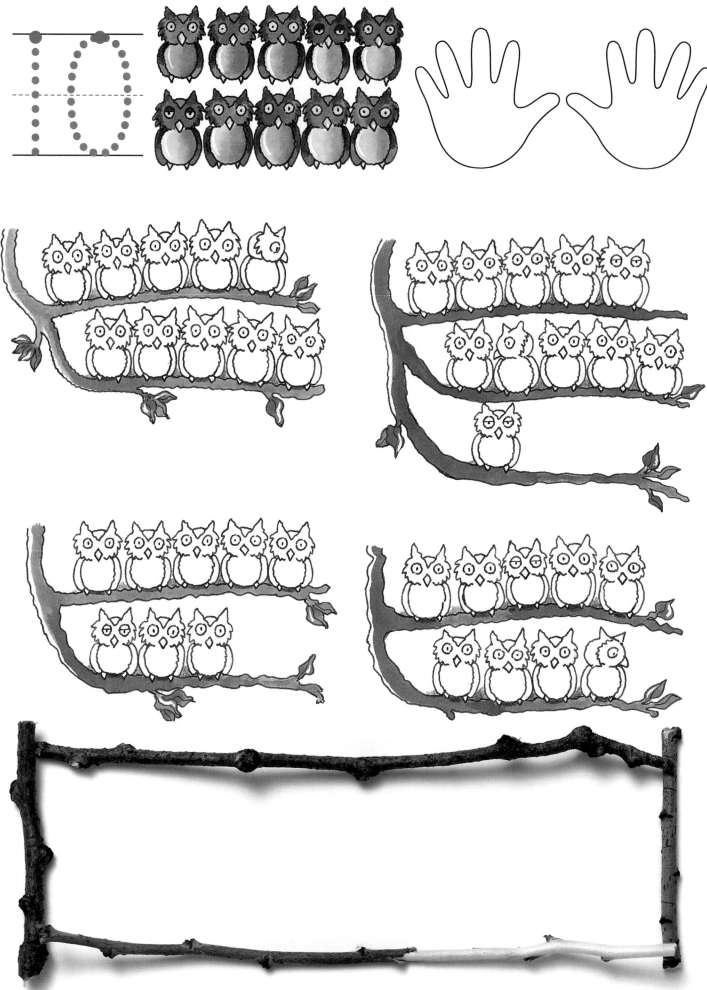

© Scott Foresman Addison Wesley

 Notes for Home: Your child colored groups fewer than 10 blue, more than 10 yellow, and equal to 10 red. Then he or she drew a group equal to 10. *Home Activity:* Ask your child to show you a group that is fewer than 10.

Name

Identify Ordinals Through Tenth

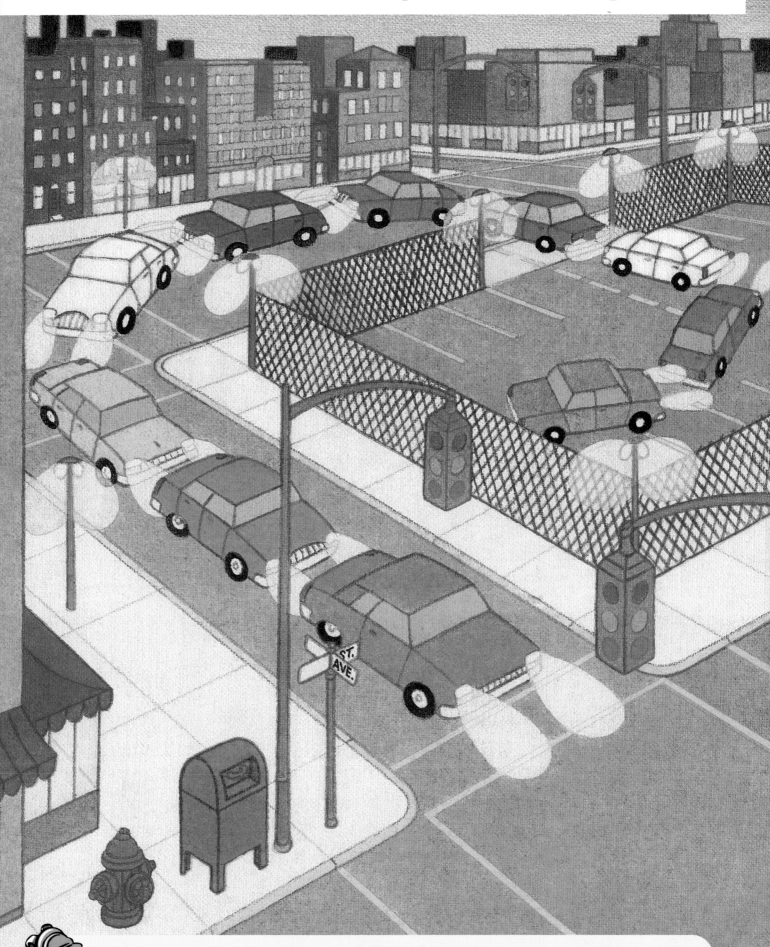

Name

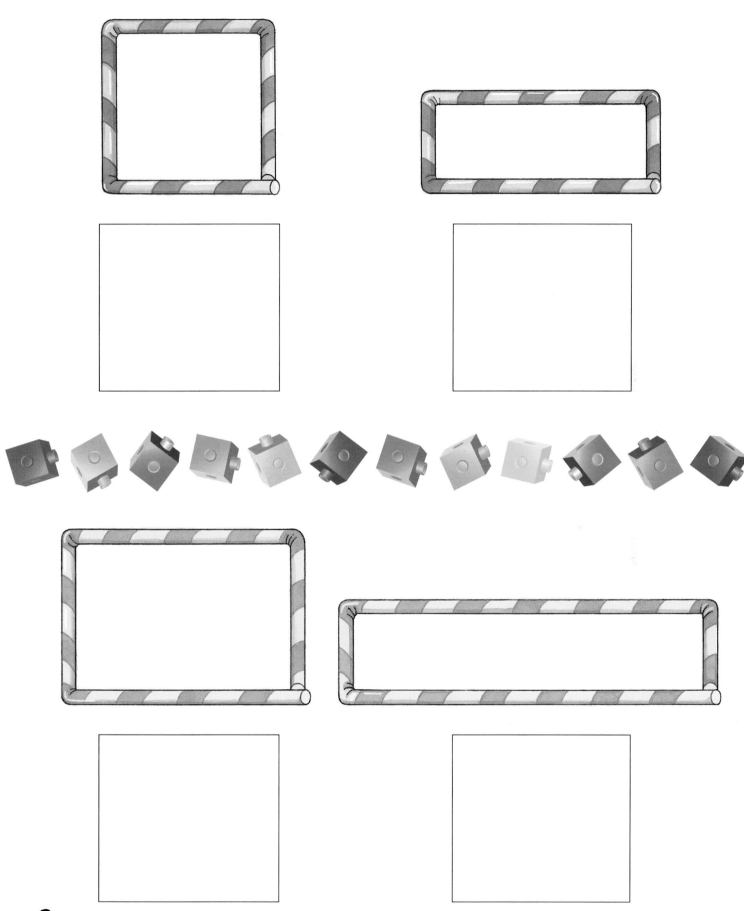

Notes for Home: Your child guessed which box in each pair holds more Snap Cubes, checked each guess, and recorded the actual numbers. *Home Activity:* Ask your child to guess and check if less than or more than 5 ice cubes will fit in a glass.

Chapter 5 Lesson 13

one hundred twenty-three   123

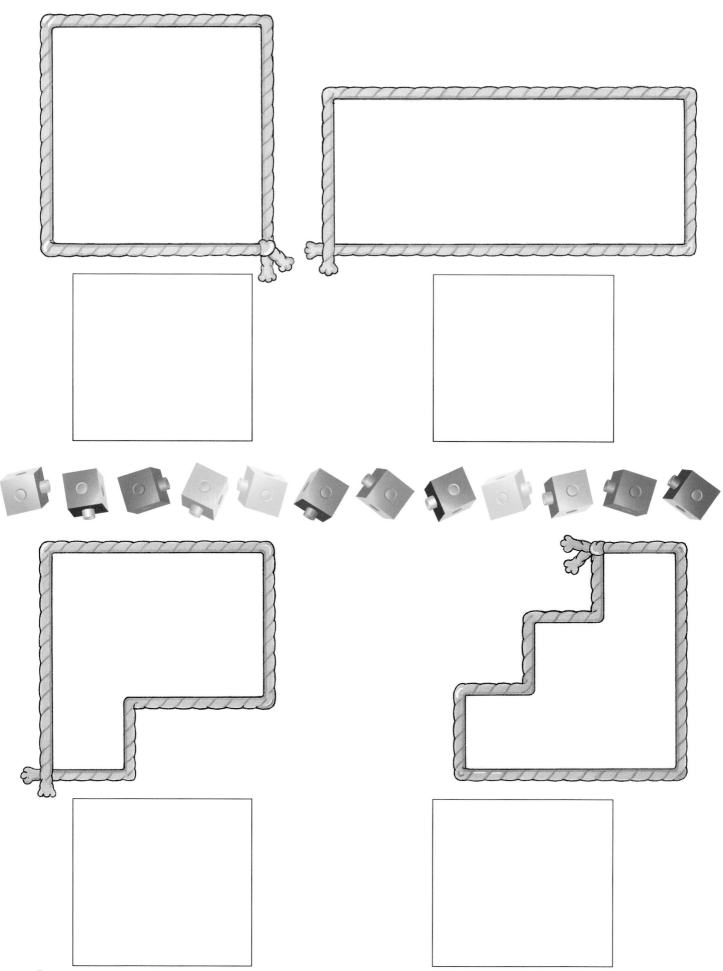

Chapter 5 Review/Test

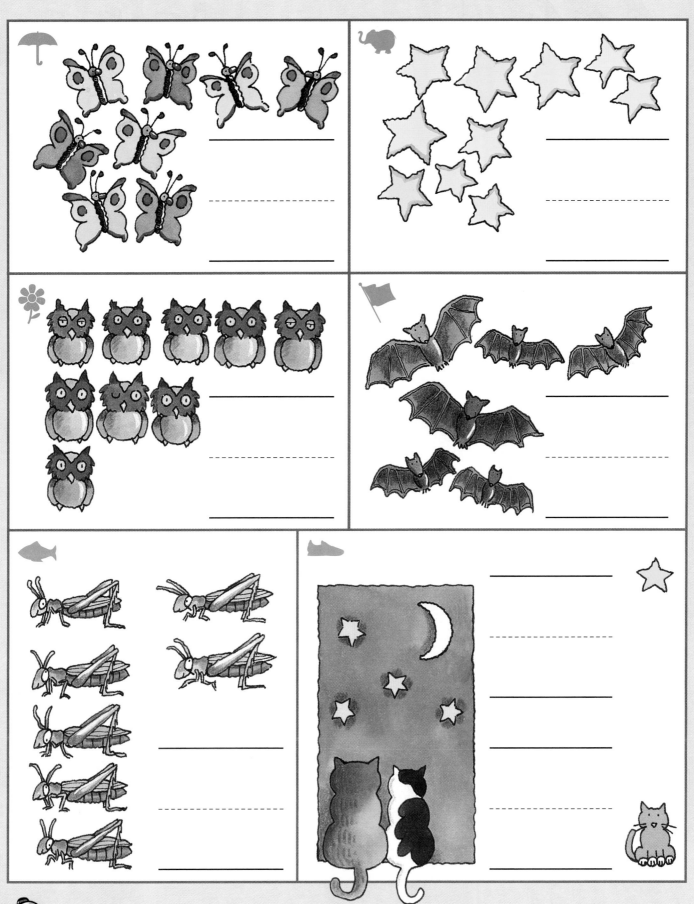

Notes for Home: Your child counted objects and wrote the number to tell how many. *Home Activity:* Ask your child to use the numbers from 6 to 10 to count objects at home, such as doors or windows.

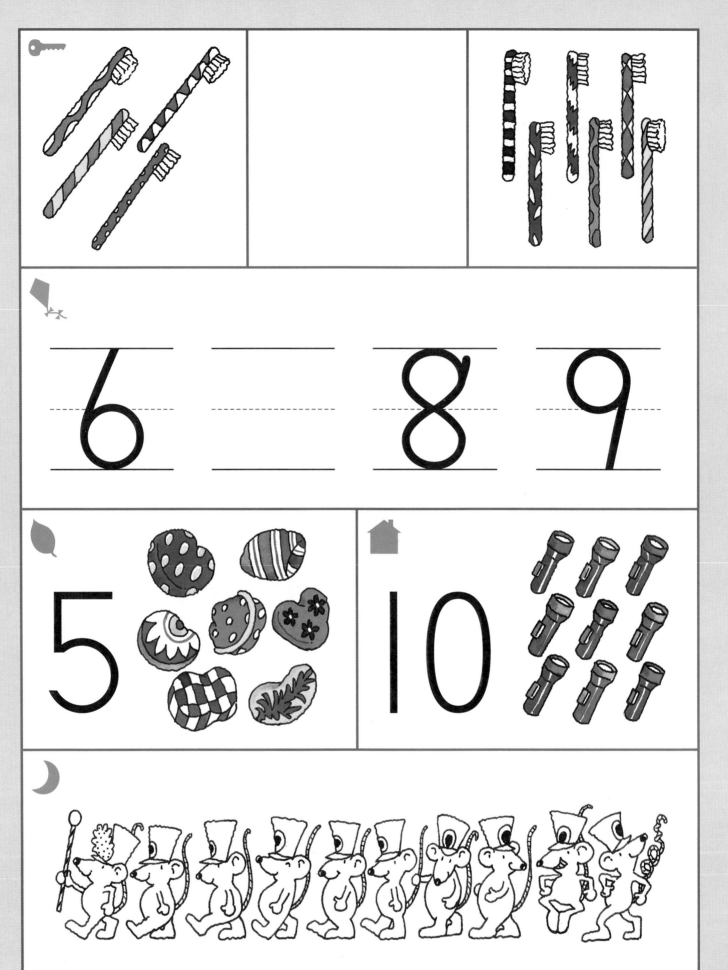

© Scott Foresman Addison Wesley

 Notes for Home: Your child drew the missing group and wrote the missing number in the sequence, compared groups to 5 and to 10, and identified the fourth and the eighth mouse. *Home Activity:* Ask your child to use ordinal numbers to tell about a group.

Dot to Dot

What You Need

Paper
Crayons

What You Do

1
Draw dots.

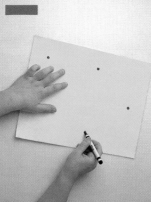

2
Check.

3
Connect.

4
Color.

Visit our Web site.
www.parent.mathsurf.com

Fold down

MathSoup

Scott Foresman - Addison Wesley   My Math Magazine   No. 5

Night Light

Night Sights

Count.
Write the number.
Follow the path from 6 to 10.

Notes for Home: Your child counted the groups, then followed the numbers in order from 6 to 10. *Home Activity:* Ask your child to count from 1 to 10 in order.

Differences

Frosted Wheats

Math at Home

Dear Family,
We will be learning how to estimate and measure how long things are, how much they weigh, and how much they can hold. I can practice by going to the grocery store with you. Here are some things we can do together.

Weigh and Measure
Hold a different fruit in each hand. Tell which is lighter and which is heavier.
Place two vegetables side-by-side. Tell which is shorter and which is longer.

Community Connection

Play a "Can you find?" game by asking your child to find a vegetable that is longer or shorter than a carrot or a fruit that is bigger or smaller than an orange.

🖥️▪🖥️ **Visit our Web site. www.parent.mathsurf.com**

Compare Lengths

 Notes for Home: Your child compared the length and height of objects. *Home Activity:* Ask your child to compare the length or height of 2 objects at home.

© Scott Foresman Addison Wesley

Name _____

Notes for Home: Your child found objects that were about 1, 5, and 10 Snap Cubes long, fit them on the page and drew pictures. *Home Activity:* Ask your child to find objects at home that are about 1, 5, and 10 paper clips long or about the length of three different objects you choose.

Chapter 6 Lesson 2   one hundred thirty-three   **133**

Notes for Home: Your child estimated the length of objects and decided which were about 1 cube, 5 cubes, or 10 cubes long. *Home Activity*: Ask your child to find an object in your home that is about 10 cubes long.

Use Numbers to Describe Length

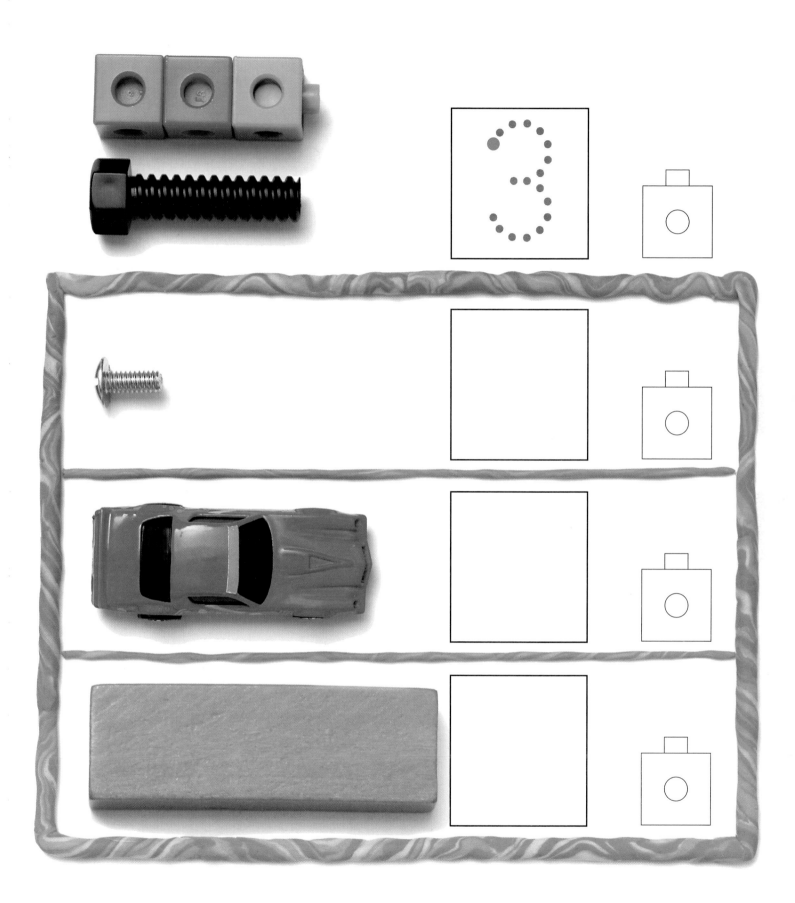

Notes for Home: Your child used and counted Snap Cubes to find the length of objects.
Home Activity: Ask your child to measure the length of an object at home with toothpicks or straws and tell you how many were used.

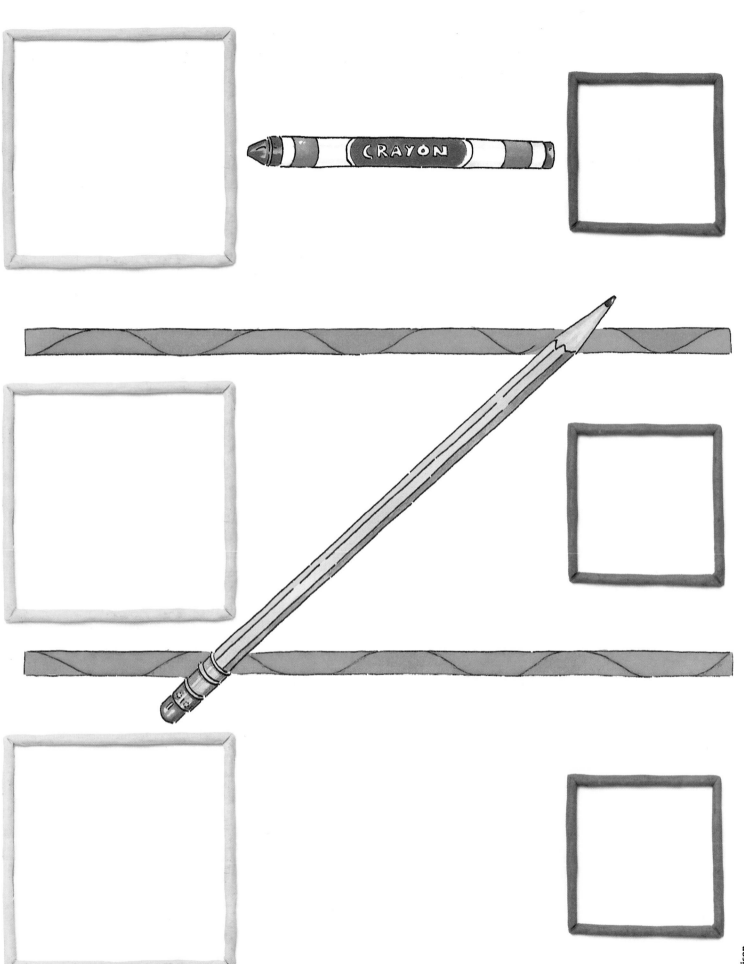

 Notes for Home: Your child chose a unit of measure, measured objects, and then wrote how many units were used. *Home Activity:* Ask your child to choose a unit of measure, such as a toothpick or paper clip, and use it to measure 3 objects.

Problem Solving: Use Objects

FRUIT

1.99

Notes for Home: Your child chose a unit of measure and used it to find the shortest path.
Home Activity: Ask your child to find a unit to measure the shortest path from one place to another place in your home.

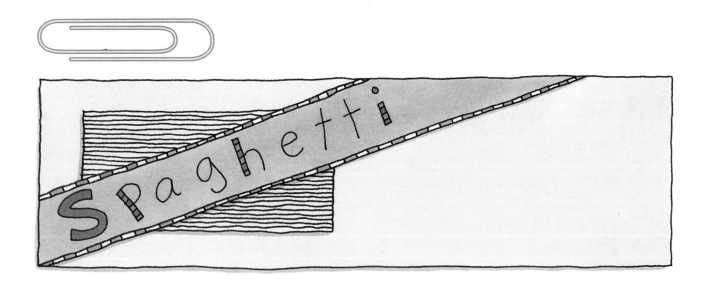

 Notes for Home: Your child measured shapes with large paper clips to find which has the longest path around it. *Home Activity:* Ask your child to walk around a sofa, a table, and a chair, then tell you which object was the longest distance around.

Name

Compare Capacities

Use Numbers to Describe Capacity

Notes for Home: Your child estimated and then tested the number of Snap Cubes that would fill different cups. *Home Activity:* Ask your child to estimate how many cereal pieces will fill a tablespoon and then count to check the estimate.

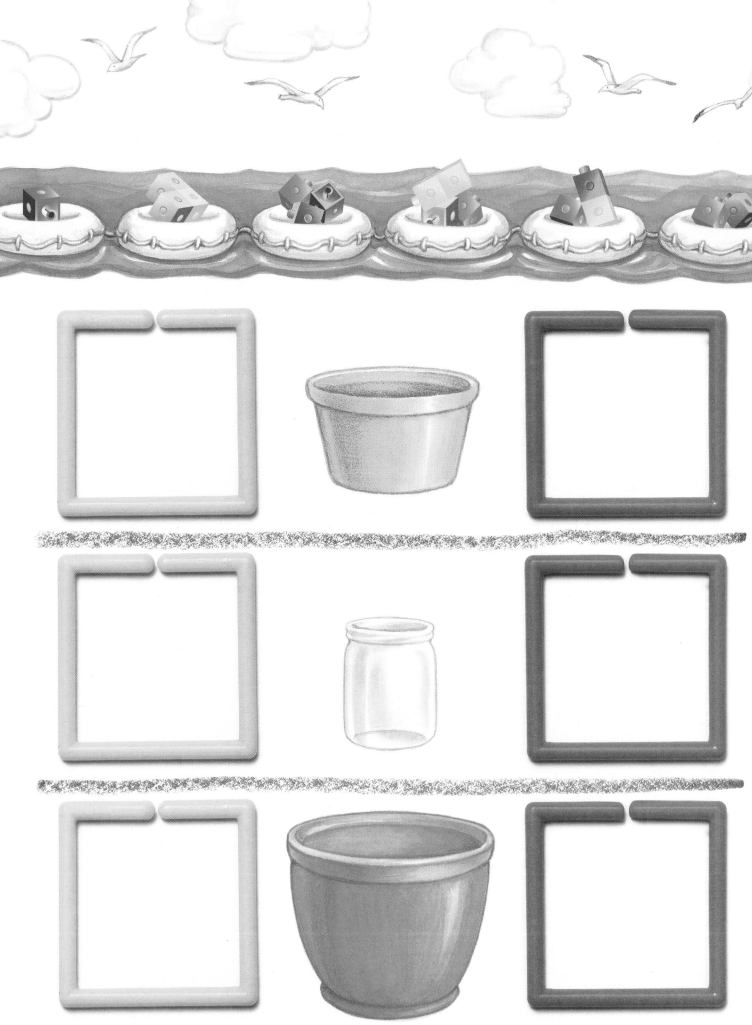

 Notes for Home: Your child estimated and tested the number of cubes it took to fill the containers. *Home Activity:* Ask your child to show you two containers and tell which one holds more.

142   one hundred forty-two

Name _____

Notes for Home: Your child used a pan balance to compare objects and recorded items of same and different weights. *Home Activity:* Help your child hold a different object in each hand to compare their weights.

 Notes for Home: Your child drew lines to show which object was about the same as, was lighter than, and was heavier than a paperback book. *Home Activity:* Ask your child to show you something that is heavier than a spoon and something that is lighter than a spoon.

Estimate Weights

 Notes for Home: Your child drew pictures to show objects that are easy to lift, that require both hands to lift, and that are too heavy to lift. *Home Activity:* Ask your child to show you something at home that is easy to lift.

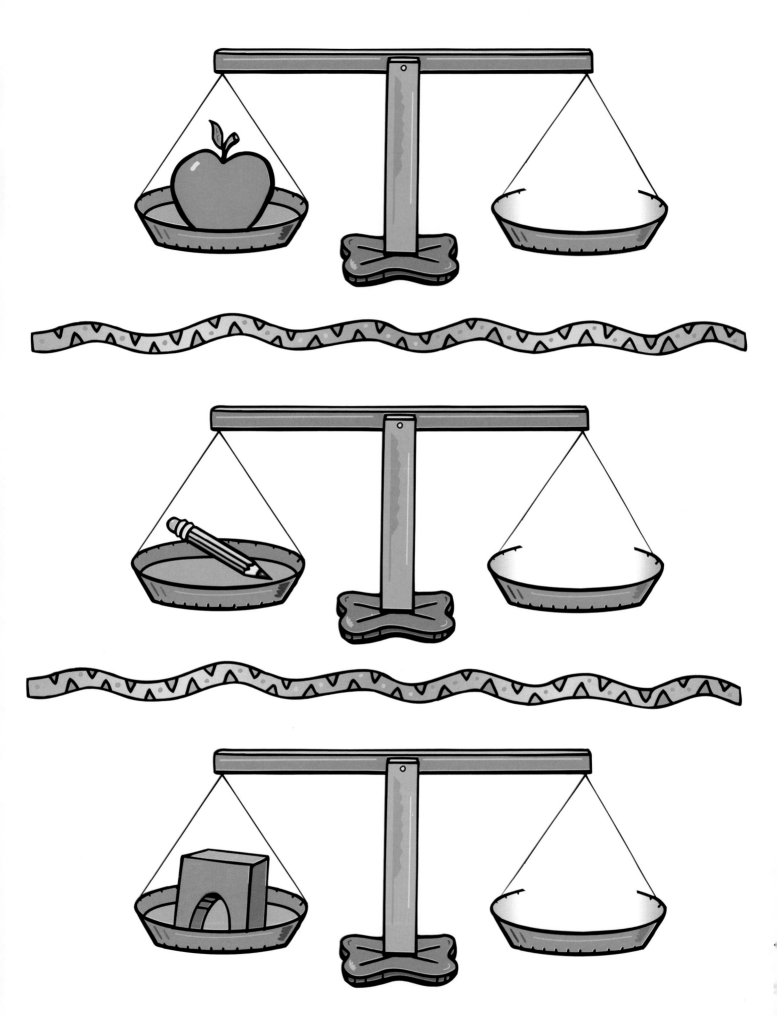

 Notes for Home: Your child drew pictures to show objects that would be about the same weight as the pictured items. *Home Activity:* Ask your child to find things at home that would be lighter or heavier than an apple.

Problem Solving: Act It Out

Notes for Home: Your child used a nonstandard measuring tool such as a serving spoon to measure the capacity of each container and determine which one holds the most. *Home Activity:* Ask your child to find a container at home that holds more than a juice glass.

Notes for Home: Help your child compare pairs of containers like those shown and circle the one that holds more. *Home Activity:* Ask your child to fill and compare other pairs of containers.

148   one hundred forty-eight

Chapter 6 Review/Test

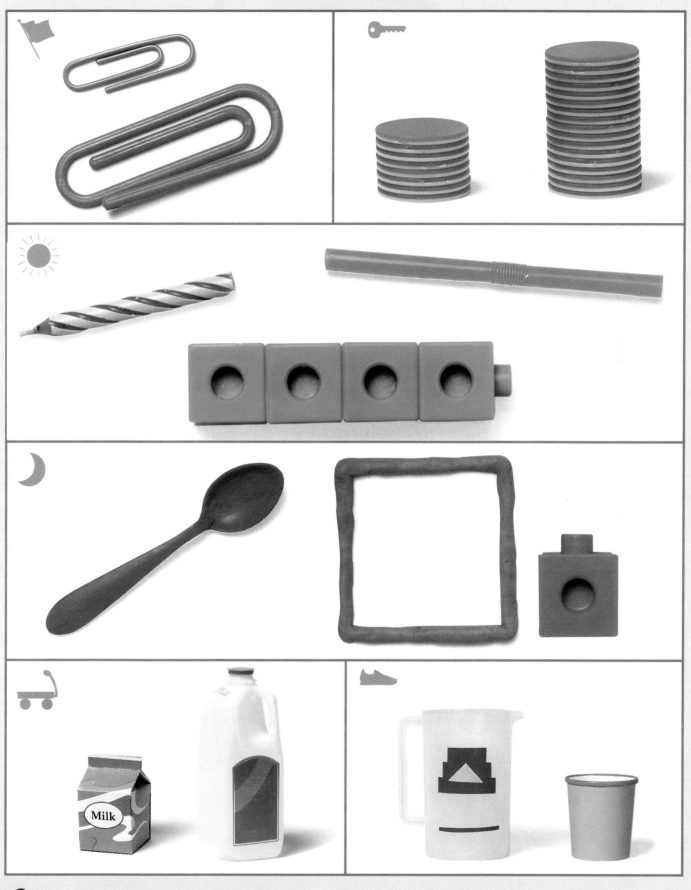

 Notes for Home: Your child circled pictures or wrote numbers to show an understanding of length and capacity. *Home Activity:* Ask your child to find two objects at home and tell which is longer.

149

Notes for Home: Your child wrote numbers, circled pictures, or drew pictures to show an understanding of capacity and weight. *Home Activity:* Ask your child to find two containers at home and tell which holds less.

Balancing Act

What You Need

Paper Punch

String

Ball

2 Cups

Tape

Hanger

Blocks

What You Do

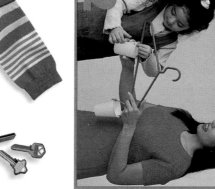

Try these too!

Fold down

MathSoup

Scott Foresman - Addison Wesley   My Math Magazine   No. 6

Treasure Hunt

Buried Treasure

Use

2 →

1 ↑

2 →

4 ↑

1 ←

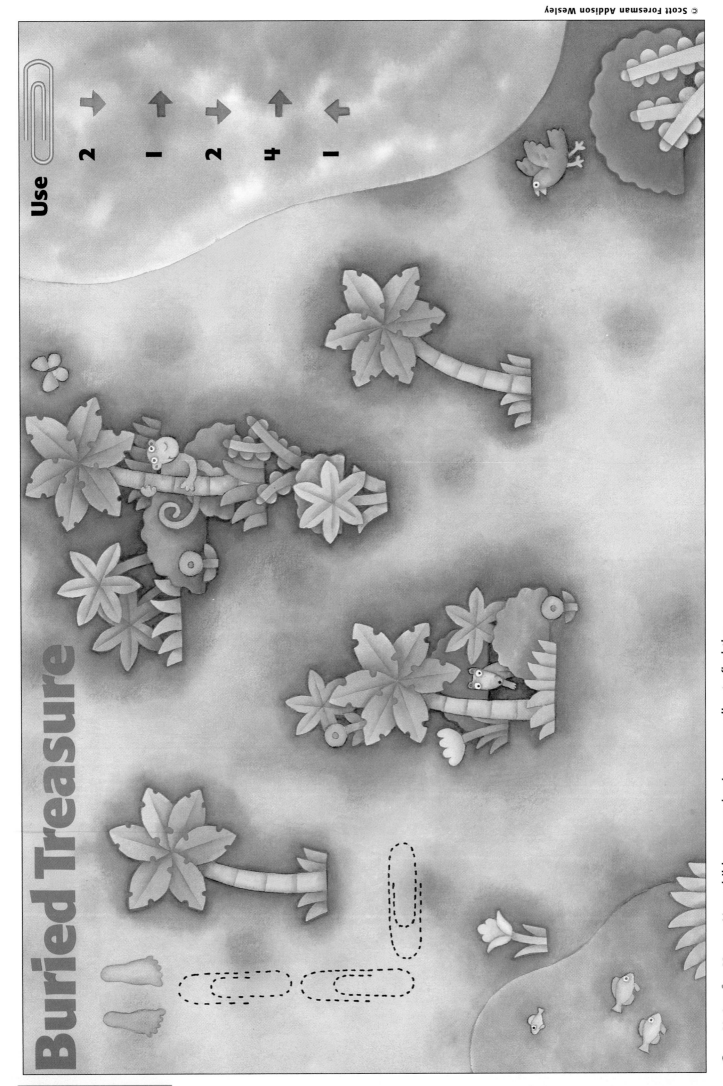

Notes for Home: Your child measured using paper clips to find the buried treasure. *Home Activity:* Ask your child to demonstrate how

Solids, Shapes, and Sharing

The Foods We Eat

Math at Home

Dear Family,

We will be learning about solids (boxes, cans, cones, pyramids, and balls), shapes (circles, triangles, squares, and rectangles), and sharing (separating groups into equal parts). I can practice what I've learned by making a shape sculpture. Here is what we can do.

Make a Shape Sculpture

1. Collect materials such as cardboard tubes, empty boxes, paper cups, and wrapping paper.
2. We can use tape or glue to put the pieces together.
3. When it is finished, we can talk about the different solids and shapes we used.

Community Connection

As you walk with your child, point out simple shapes seen in the environment. Rectangular doors and windows, wheels that are circular and structures that contain triangles are examples.

🖳🖳 **Visit our Web site.** www.parent.mathsurf.com

Explore Solids

Find.

 Notes for Home: Your child found objects that were the same shape as boxes, cans, cones, pyramids, and balls. *Home Activity:* Help your child find box-shaped objects at home.

Circle.

 Notes for Home: Your child circled the objects that are about the same shape as the solids. *Home Activity:* Ask your child to find a box, a ball, and a can, and then tell how they are alike and how they are different.

Sort Solids

Draw.

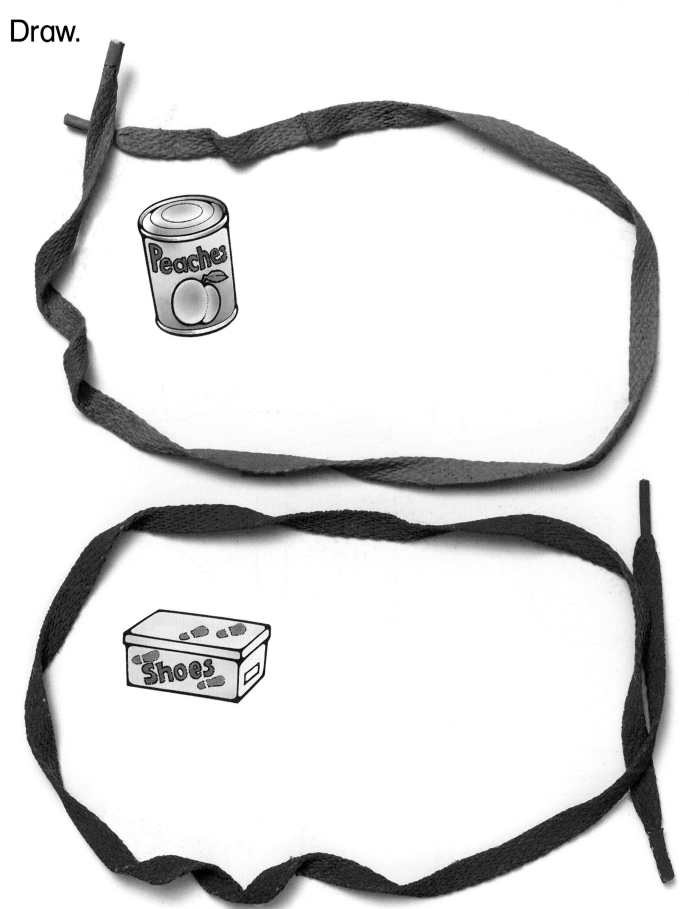

Notes for Home: Your child drew pictures of things similiar to the can and the box, and explained how the objects were alike. *Home Activity:* Help your child find other objects that have shapes like the can and the box, and discuss their similarities.

Chapter 7 Lesson 2   one hundred fifty-seven   **157**

orange

blue

Color.

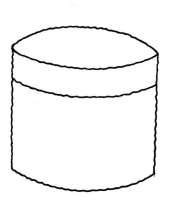
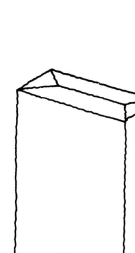
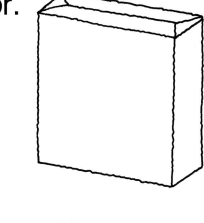
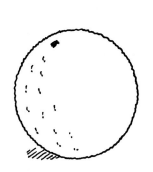

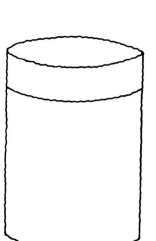

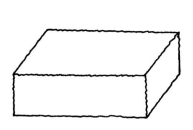

Notes for Home: Your child colored box-shaped objects yellow, ball-shaped objects orange, and can-shaped objects blue. *Home Activity:* Ask your child to find pairs of same-shaped objects at home.

Find Shapes in Solids

Circle one.

 Notes for Home: Your child circled one solid, then made shape prints from the face of that solid. *Home Activity:* Ask your child to tell you how to make shape prints. Then look for similar shapes at home.

Chapter 7 Lesson 3   one hundred fifty-nine   159

Color.

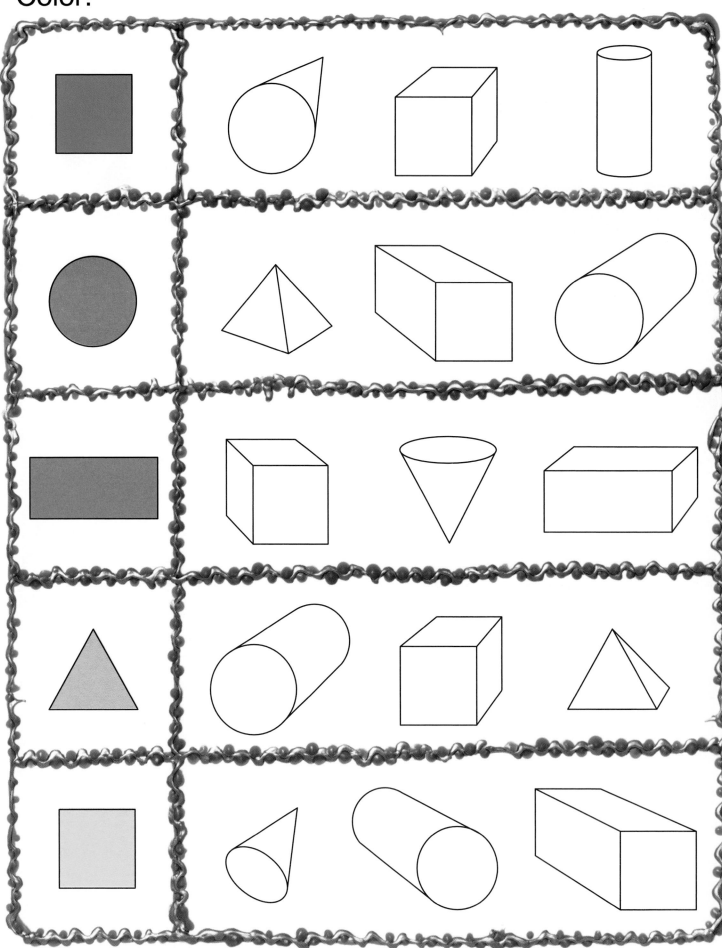

 Notes for Home: Your child colored the face on each solid that matched the stamp print in each row. *Home Activity:* Help your child trace a circle from a can.

Name _____

Paste.

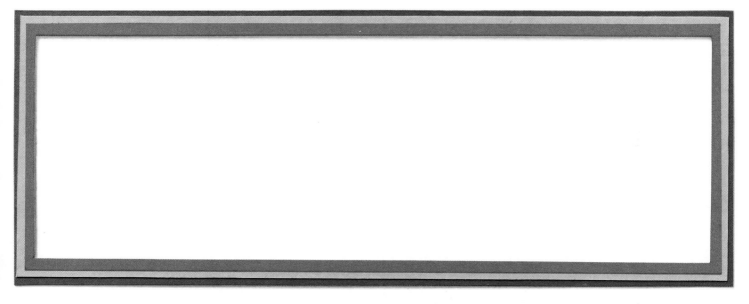

 Notes for Home: Your child made squares and other rectangles. *Home Activity:* Ask your child to show you a rectangle and tell how many corners and sides it has.

Color.

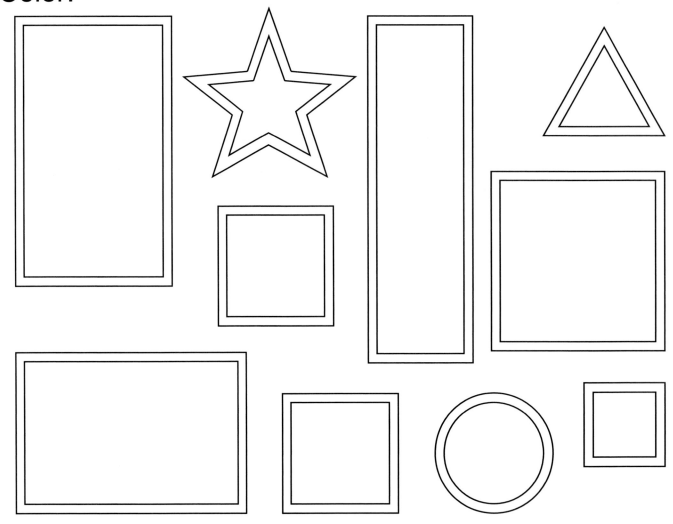

Draw.

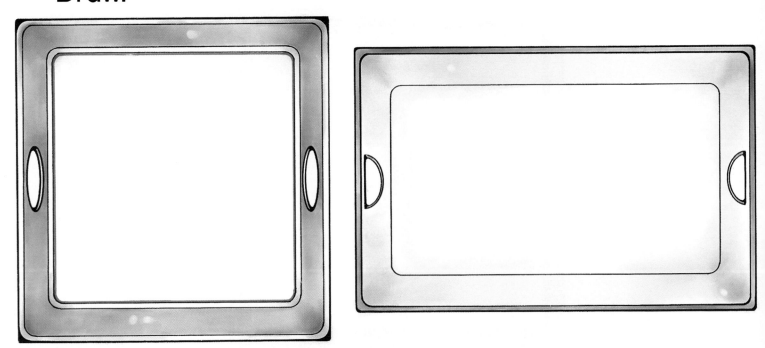

Notes for Home: Your child colored all the rectangles yellow, outlined those that are squares in red, and then drew square and rectangular crackers. *Home Activity:* Ask your child to point out rectangular shapes in your home and tell which ones are squares.

Explore Circles and Triangles

Make.

Notes for Home: Your child worked with others to make circles and triangles with their bodies, and then drew circles and triangles. *Home Activity:* Ask your child to use fingers and thumbs to make circles and triangles.

Draw.

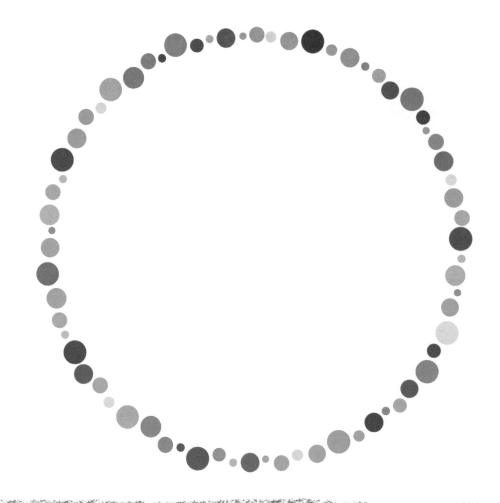

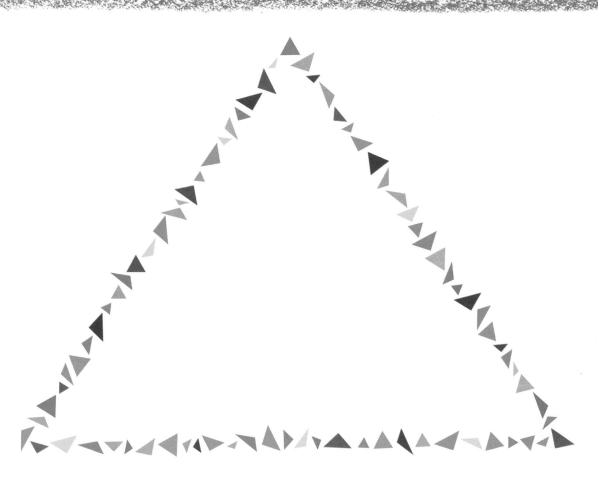

 Notes for Home: Your child drew circular objects in the top frame and triangular objects in the bottom frame. *Home Activity:* Help your child find circular and triangular objects around your home.

Combine and Separate Shapes

Cover.

Notes for Home: Your child covered large shapes with smaller shapes, then drew lines to show the smaller shapes. *Home Activity:* Give your child 4 rectangular pieces of paper. Ask him or her to search for something that can be covered with 2 or more of the pieces.

Chapter 7 Lesson 6   one hundred sixty-five   165

Place. Paste.

 Notes for Home: Your child arranged cut-out shapes to make new shapes, then pasted them in a favorite arrangement to make a shape picture. *Home Activity:* Help your child make shape pictures from round, square, and triangular shapes.

Problem Solving: Using Objects

Cover. Color.

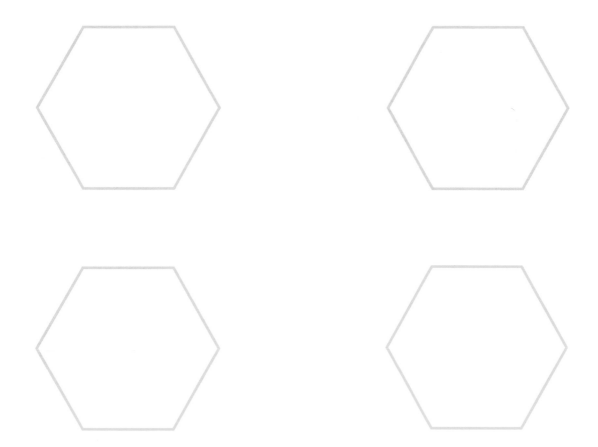

Notes for Home: Your child used pattern blocks to show different ways to cover the same shape.
Home Activity: Ask your child to use string or toothpicks to make different shapes.

Cover. Color.

Notes for Home: Your child used pattern blocks to cover the tree trunk, the path, and the apple.
Home Activity: Ask your child to show you how smaller shapes may be used to create one big shape.

Equal Parts

Paste.

2

3

4

Circle.

 Notes for Home: Your child circled the foods that show equal parts. *Home Activity:* Ask your child to help prepare and serve a snack or meal by making equal portions.

Identify Halves

Paste.

Notes for Home: Your child investigated different ways to cut a sandwich in half.
Home Activity: Ask your child to help you cut a sandwich or another type of food in half and tell what new shapes are made.

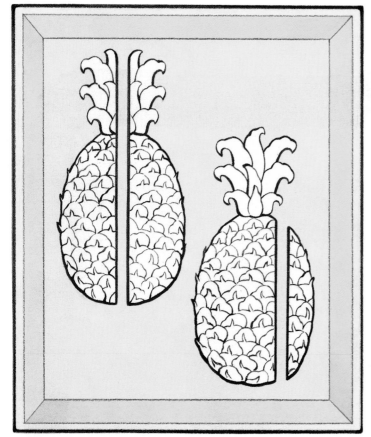

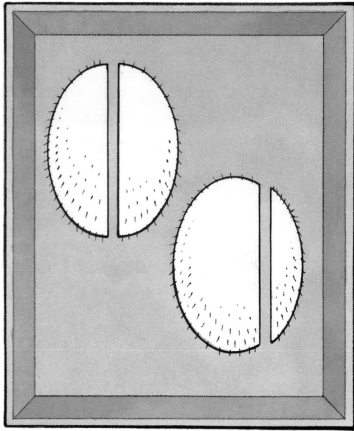

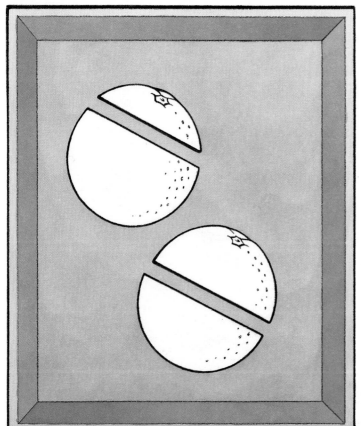

 Notes for Home: Have your child decide which piece of fruit in each box shows halves and indicate the choice by coloring one half of each. *Home Activity:* Ask your child to divide foods like bananas, muffins, and sandwiches into equal parts.

Make Equal Groups

Draw. Share.

2

4

6

8

10

 Notes for Home: Your child circled a number and used counters to show two equal groups.
Home Activity: Ask your child to use buttons, pennies, or other small objects to show two equal groups of 6.

Chapter 7 Lesson 10   one hundred seventy-three   **173**

Draw.

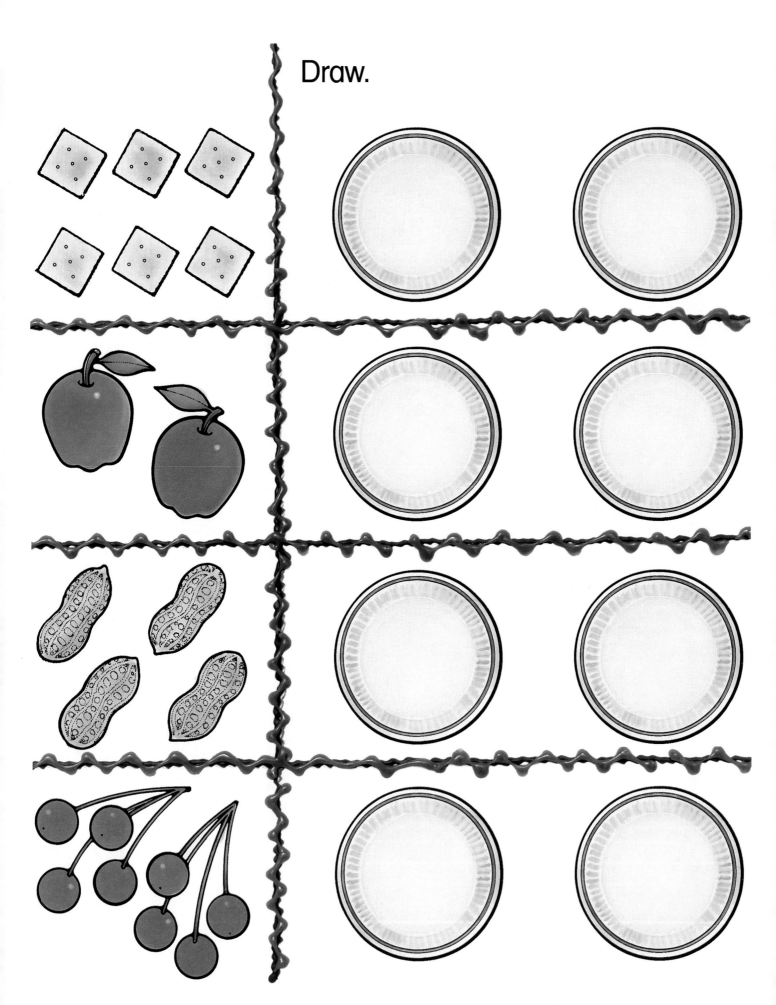

Problem Solving: Draw a Picture

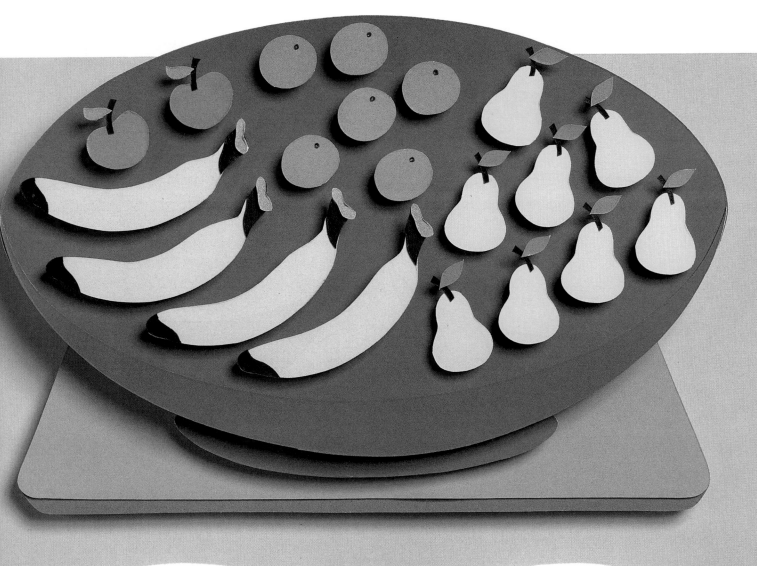

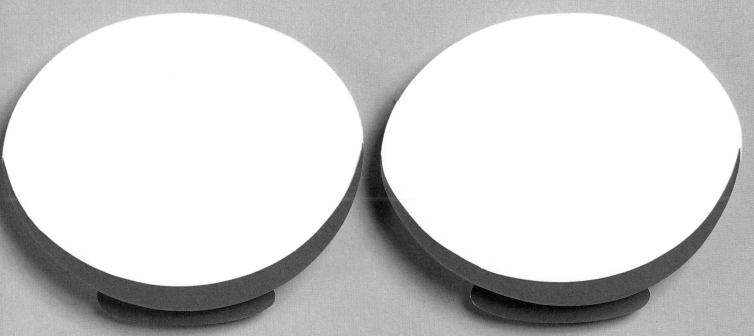

 Notes for Home: Your child drew pictures to figure out how the foods could be shared equally. *Home Activity:* Ask your child to draw a picture to show how 6 rice cakes could be shared equally between 2 people.

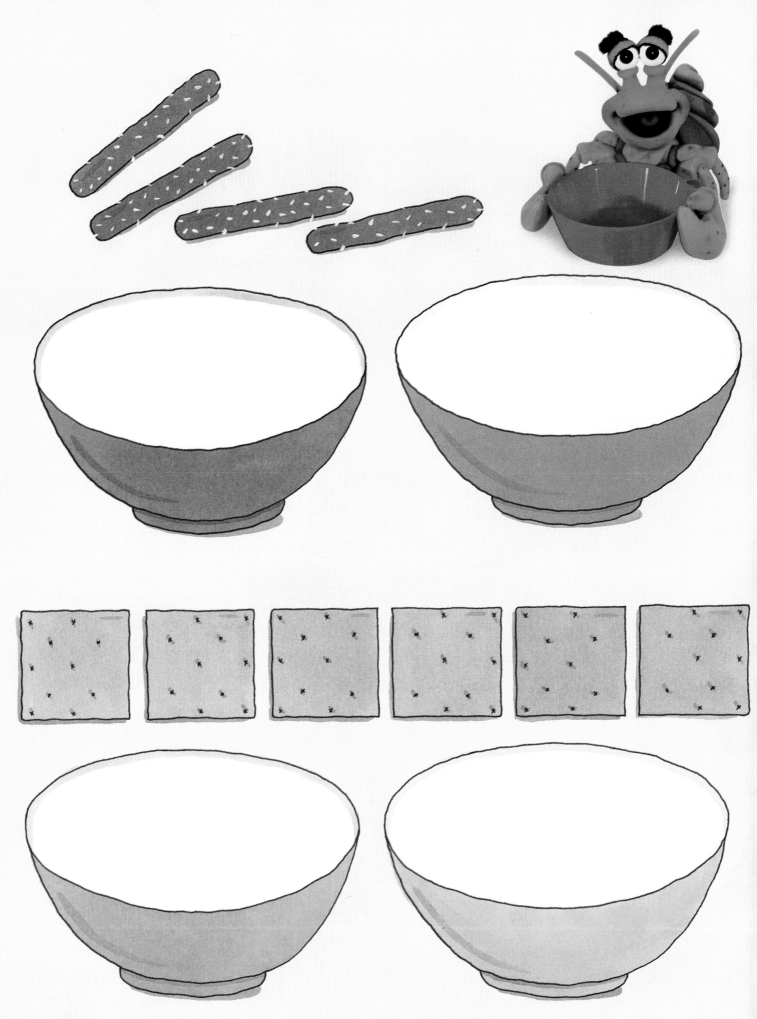

Notes for Home: Your child drew pictures to show fair shares. *Home Activity:* Ask your child to make a fair-share portion for each of you, the next time you have a snack together.

176   one hundred seventy-six

Chapter 7 Review/Test

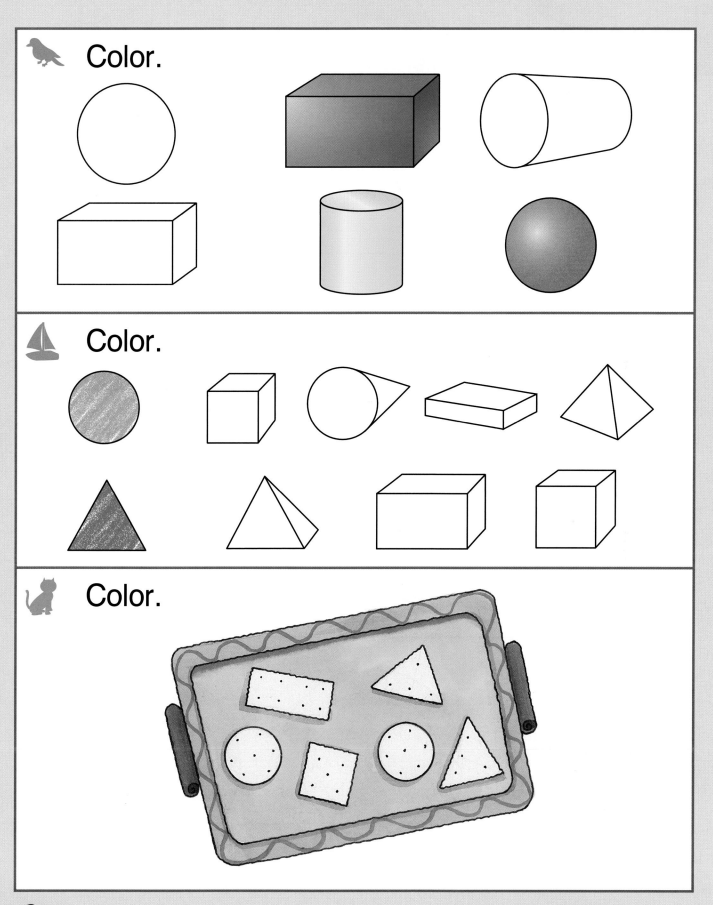

Color.

Color.

Color.

Notes for Home: Your child followed specific directions to show an understanding of solids and shapes. *Home Activity:* Ask your child to find solids and shapes at home that match the solids and shapes on this page.

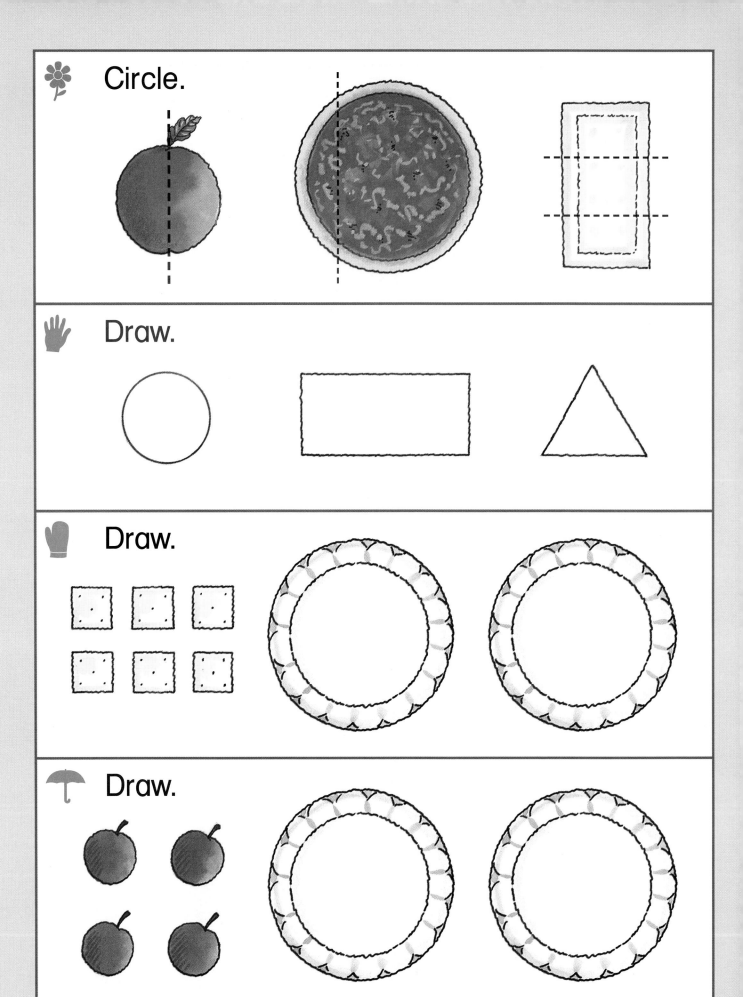

Circle.

Draw.

Draw.

Draw.

 Notes for Home: Your child followed specific directions to show an understanding of equal parts and equal groups. *Home Activity:* Ask your child to divide a food item at home into two fair shares.

Baking Biscuits

What You Need

1 cup flour   3 tsp. baking powder

1/2 tsp. salt   1/4 cup margarine

1/2 cup milk

1/2 cup raisins

What You Do

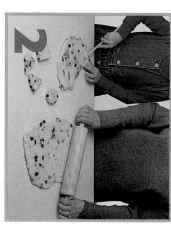

1

2

3

4

Fold down

MathSoup

Scott Foresman - Addison Wesley   My Math Magazine   No. 7

**Find
Shapes
and
Solids**

Find these shapes and solids.

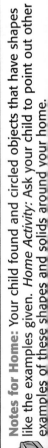

Scene Search

Math Fun

Pretzels

Crackers

Frozen Yogurt

Just for Fun

Dear Family,

We will be learning how to make numbers to 10 in different ways, and we will use numbers to 20 to count and measure. I can practice making numbers to 10 in different ways when we eat a fruit. Here is what we can do:

Seed Count
Pick a fruit that has seeds, such as an apple, orange, or grapefruit.
Cut the fruit in half.
We can count the seeds in one half.
We can count the seeds in the other half.
We can count all the seeds together.

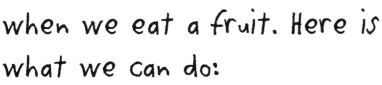

Community Connection

Plan a visit to the children's room of a neighborhood library. Look for displays of books that have numbers on the covers. Then, pick one or two books to read together at the library or at home.

  **Visit our Web site. www.parent.mathsurf.com**

Represent Numbers to 10

Draw. Write.

Notes for Home: Your child drew circles in the ten-frames to show the number of objects in each picture. *Home Activity:* Have your child draw a ten-frame and use objects to show the number of fingers you hold up.

Draw. Write.

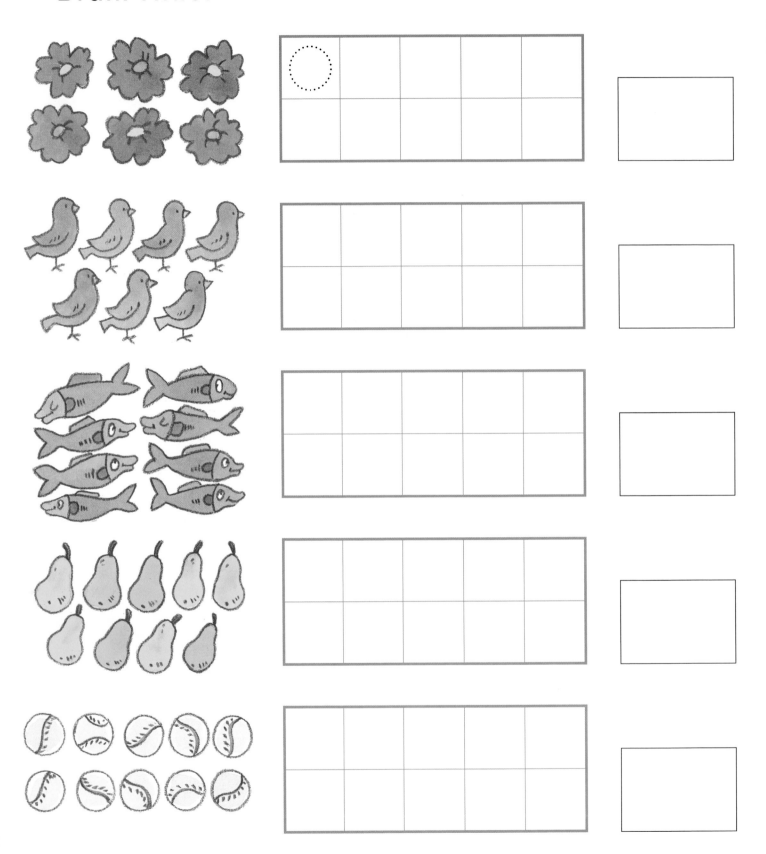

184   one hundred eighty-four

Color.

Notes for Home: Your child used red and yellow counters to show different ways to make 3.
Home Activity: Ask your child to use two kinds of objects to make three, for example: 2 pennies and
1 button; three cereal pieces; etc.

Color.

Notes for Home: Your child used red and yellow counters and colored to show different ways to make 4.
Home Activity: Ask your child to use both sides of 4 pennies to make different arrangements of 4.

186   one hundred eighty-six

Name _____

Color. Write.

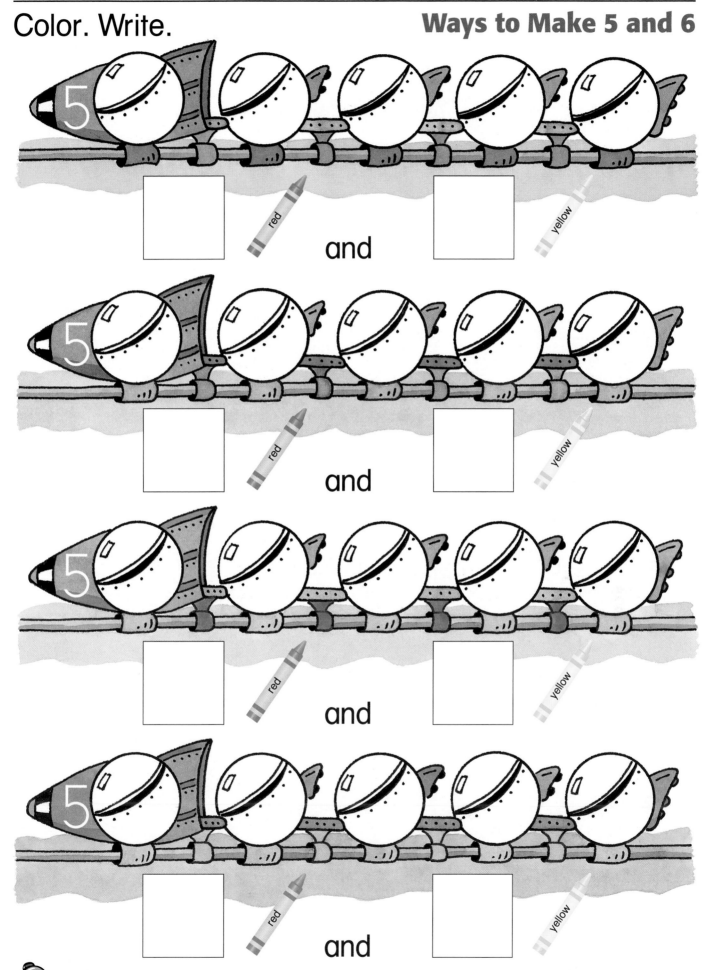

and

and

and

and

![backpack] **Notes for Home:** Your child colored to show different ways to make 5.
Home Activity: Ask your child to use groups of forks and spoons to show 5.

Color. Write.

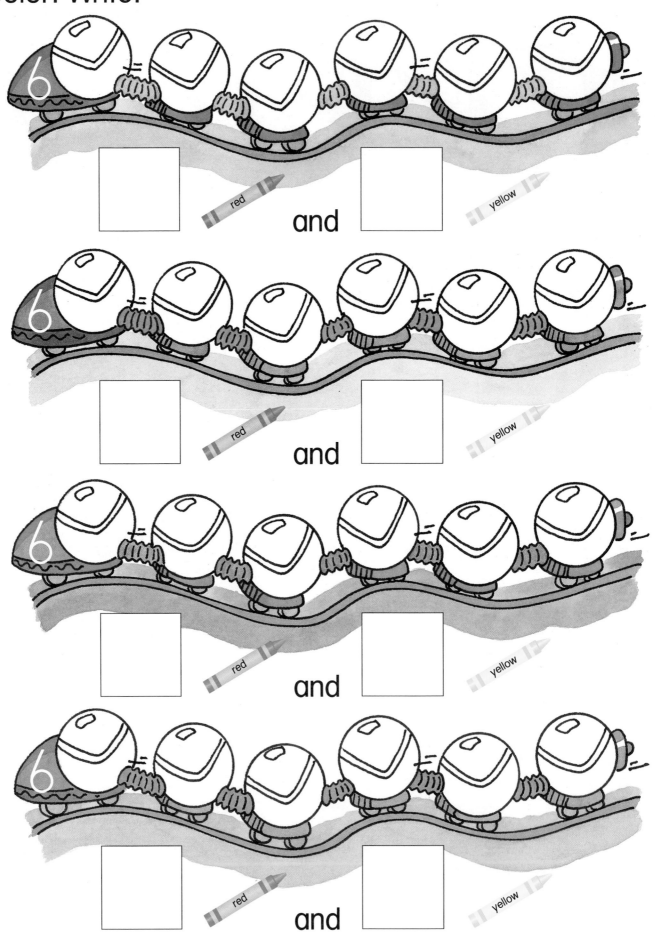

and

and

and

and

Notes for Home: Your child colored to show different ways to make 6.
Home Activity: Ask your child to use two different pasta shapes to make 6.

Color.

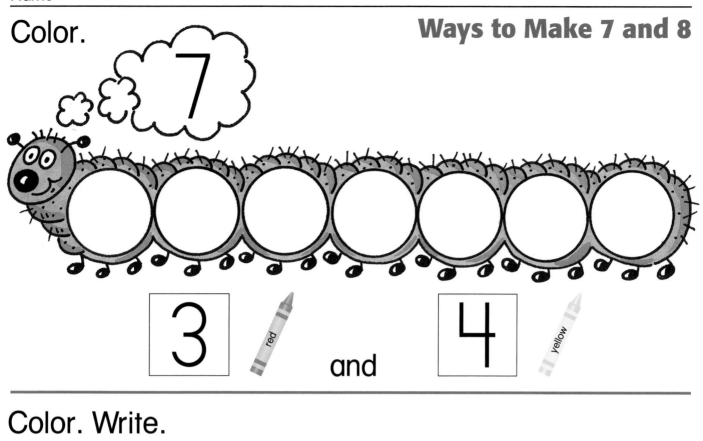

3 and 4

red yellow

Color. Write.

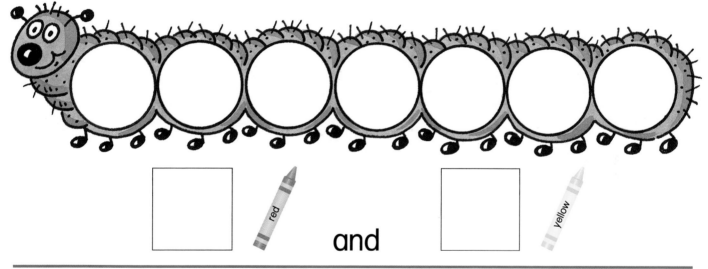

and

red yellow

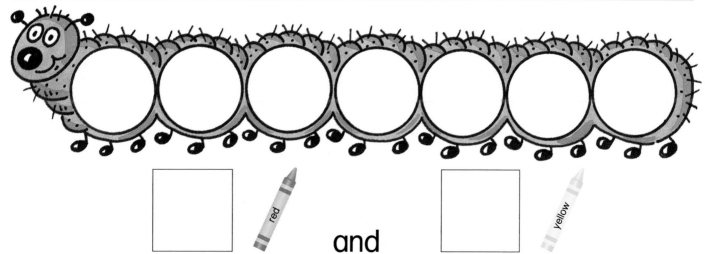

and

red yellow

Notes for Home: Your child colored to show different ways to make 7.
Home Activity: Ask your child to use two different kinds of fruit to make 7.

Color.

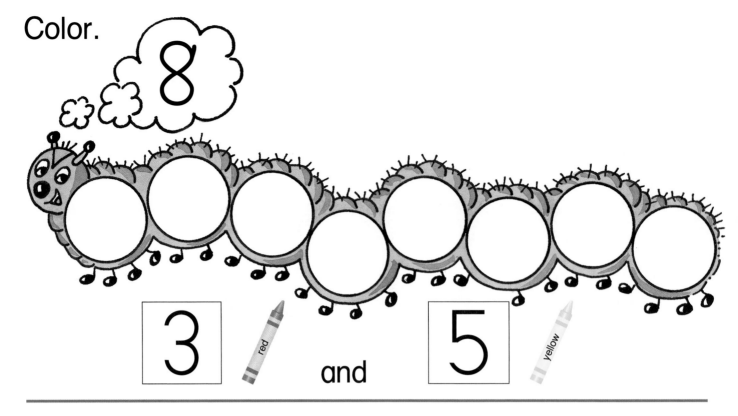

3 red and 5 yellow

Color. Write.

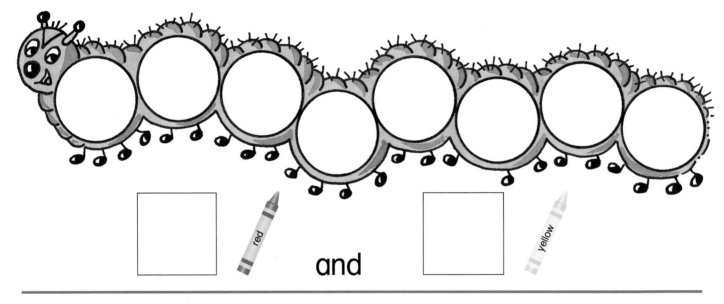

and

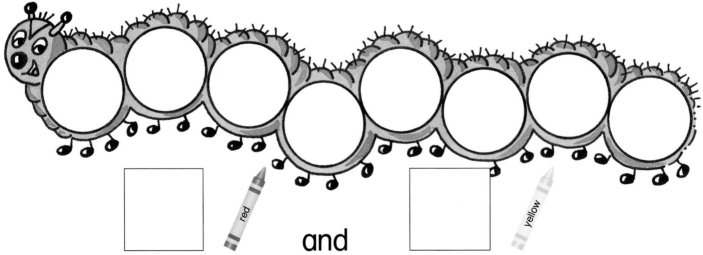

and

Notes for Home: Your child colored to show different ways to make 8.
Home Activity: Ask your child to use 2 colors to draw a picture of a funny creature with 8 sections.

Ways to Make 9 and 10

Count. Write.

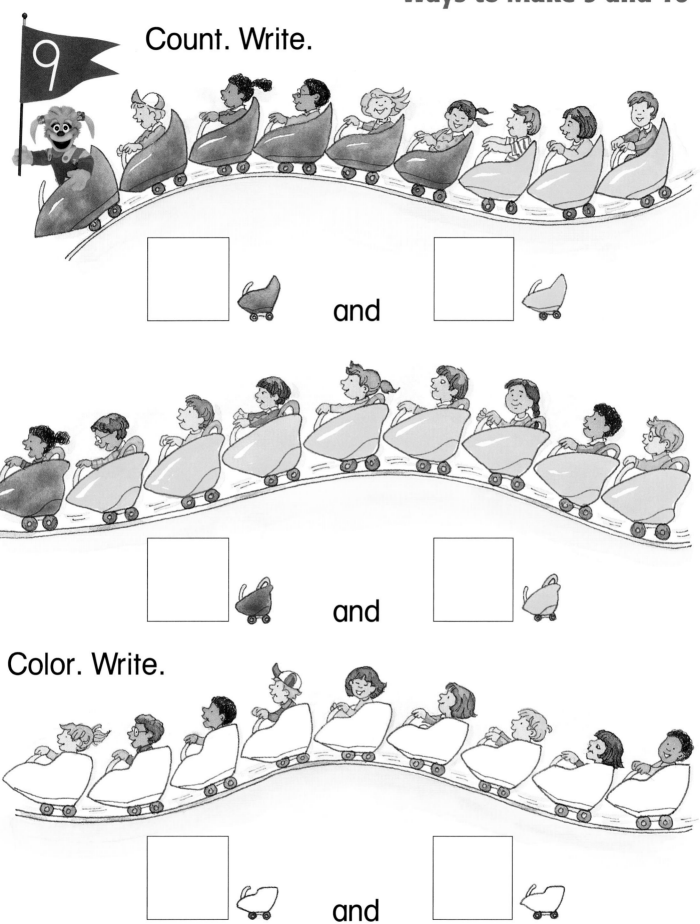

☐ and ☐

☐ and ☐

Color. Write.

☐ and ☐

Notes for Home: Your child recorded some ways to make 9. *Home Activity:* Ask your child to use two kinds of beans or other small objects to show ways to make 9.

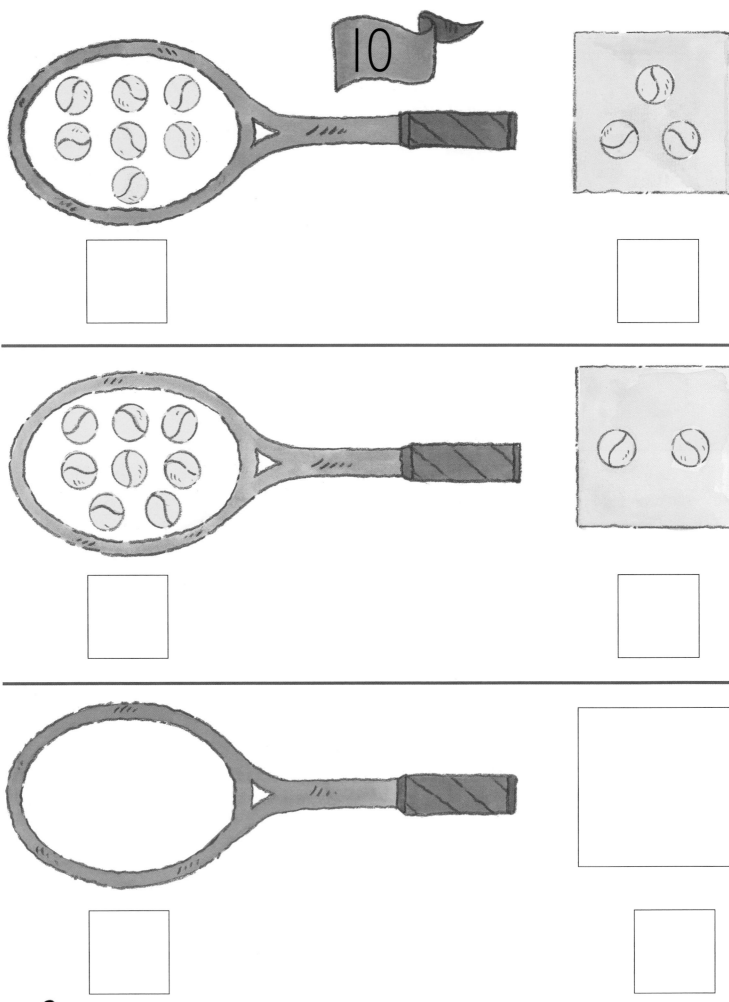

Notes for Home: Your child recorded different ways to make 10. *Home Activity:* Ask your child to draw red and blue circles to show another way to make 10.

192   one hundred ninety-two

Problem Solving: Look for a Pattern

 Notes for Home: Your child found a pattern and continued it by coloring the flags blue and red. *Home Activity:* Ask your child to look for color patterns around your home.

Write.

Draw.

Notes for Home: Your child wrote numbers to describe the pattern and drew circles and/or triangles to continue the pattern. *Home Activity:* Ask your child to match this pattern using pennies and nickels.

Draw. Count.

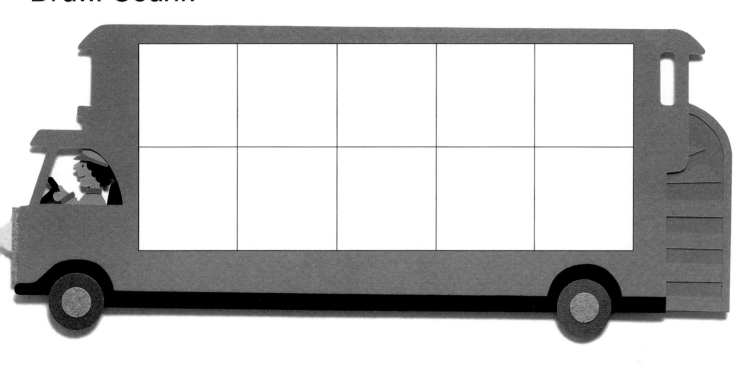

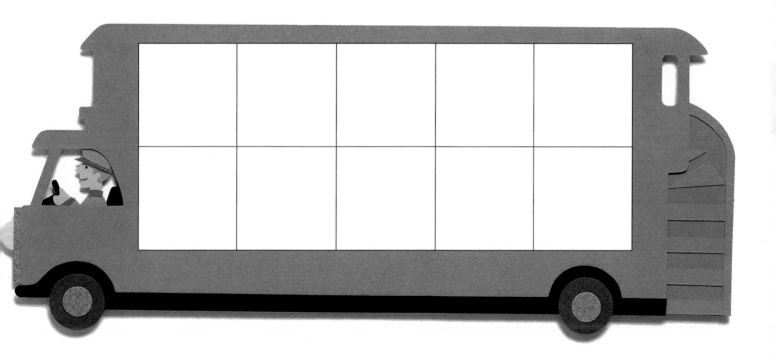

0 1 2 3 4 5 6 7 8 9 10 11 12 13 14 15 16 17 18 19 20

 Notes for Home: Your child counted groups of up to 20 objects. *Home Activity:* Ask your child to count a group of 20 pennies.

Draw.

12

20

18

15

Notes for Home: Your child showed numbers more than 10 on the double ten-frames.
Home Activity: Ask your child to show each number on this page with small snacks such as grapes, peanuts, or crackers.

Name _____

Estimate and Verify Capacity and Weight

Estimate: More than 10 🎲
Fewer than 10 🎲

Measure.

Estimate: More than 10 🎲
Fewer than 10 🎲

Draw.

Measure.

Notes for Home: Your child estimated and measured capacity. *Home Activity:* Decide on a measuring tool such as a small cup. Show your child a container, and talk about whether it would take more or fewer than 10 cups to fill it.

Estimate: More than 10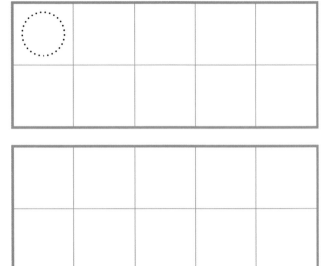
Fewer than 10

Measure.

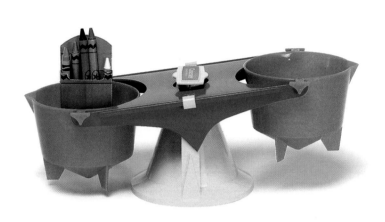

Estimate: More than 10
Draw. Fewer than 10

Measure.

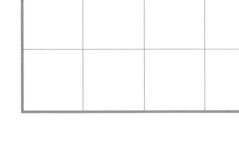

 Notes for Home: Your child used a pan balance to estimate and compare weight.
Home Activity: Ask your child to point out people weighing fruits and vegetables the next time you shop for food.

Estimate and Verify Length

Estimate: More than 10

               Fewer than 10

Draw.

Measure.

Estimate: More than 10

               Fewer than 10

Draw.

Measure.

Notes for Home: Your child estimated and measured length. *Home Activity:* Ask your child to estimate whether his or her shoe is more than or fewer than 10 pennies long. Then measure the shoe with pennies to check.

Find something longer than 10 🖉.
Draw.

Measure.

Find something shorter than 10 🖉.
Draw.

Measure.

Notes for Home: Have your child draw pictures of things he or she estimates are longer than and shorter than 10 paper clips. Then help your child measure to check his or her estimates. *Home Activity:* Have your child estimate land check whether a favorite toy is longer or shorter than 10 pennies.

Problem Solving: Draw a Picture

Draw legs.

Notes for Home: Your child drew legs on the animals and told if they had more or fewer than 10 legs all together. *Home Activity:* Ask your child to draw a make-believe animal with 20 legs.

Name _____

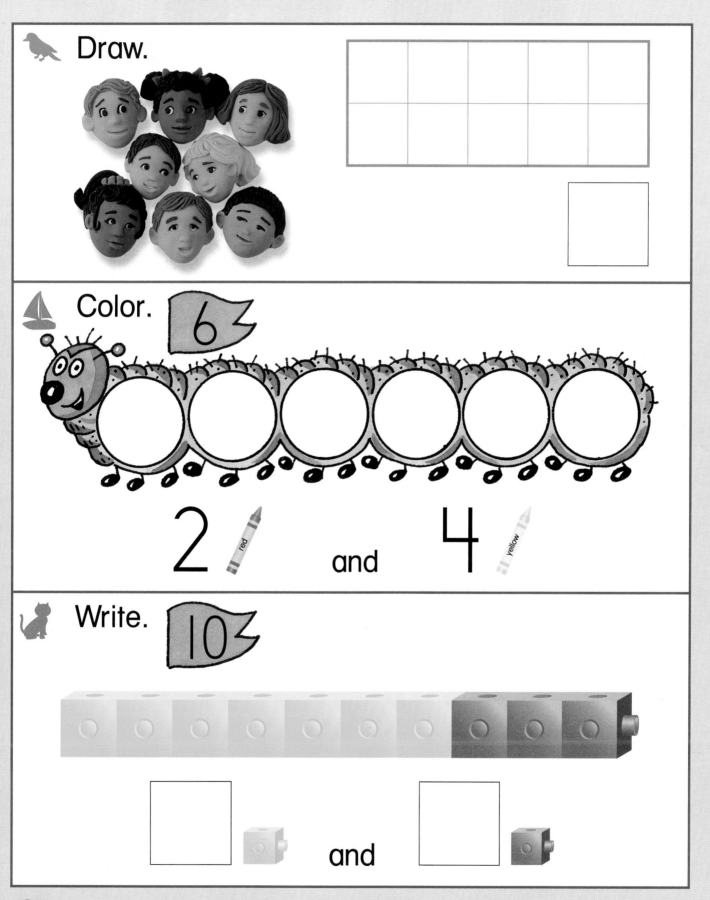

Draw.

Color. 6

2 _red_ and 4 _yellow_

Write. 10

☐ and ☐

Notes for Home: Your child matched numbers and showed ways to make numbers. *Home Activity:* Ask your child to describe how the caterpillar shows 6.

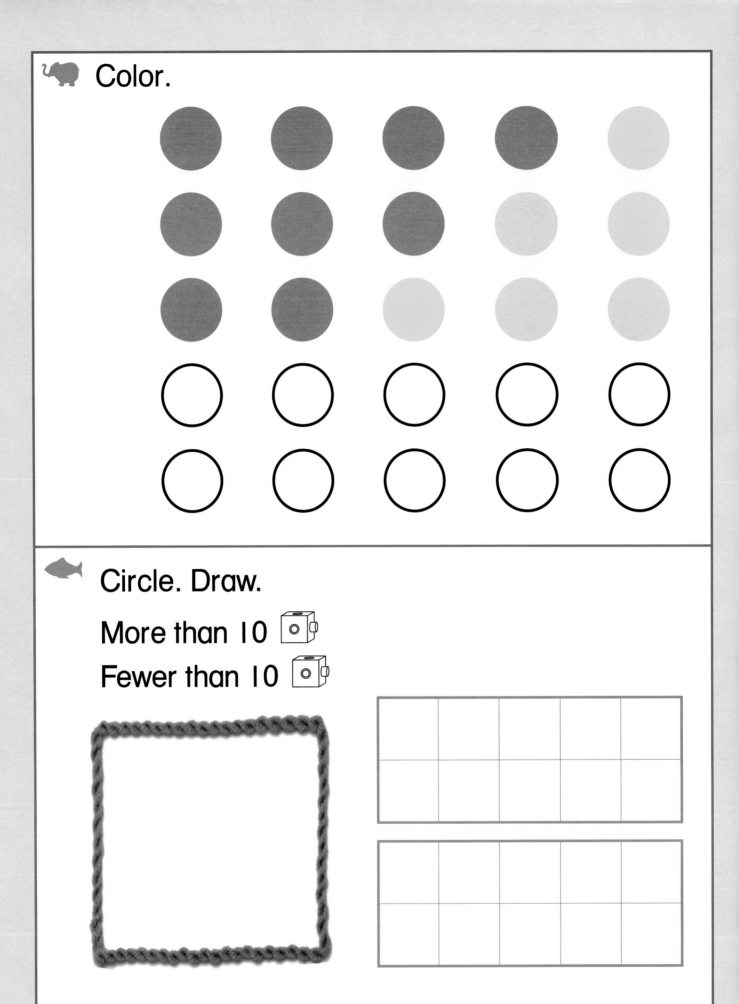

Color.

Circle. Draw.

More than 10

Fewer than 10

Notes for Home: Your child continued a pattern and estimated and measured the length of an object.
Home Activity: Help your child arrange 10 pennies and 10 nickels in four rows of 5 to make a stair-step pattern.

Bowl O'Rama

What You Need

10 Plastic Bottles

1 Ball   Pencil and Paper

What You Do

1
Set up the bottles.

2
Roll the ball.

3
Score.

4
Play again.

Fold down

Math Soup

Scott Foresman - Addison Wesley   My Math Magazine   No. 8

Play with the Animals

Farm Fun

Draw spots.

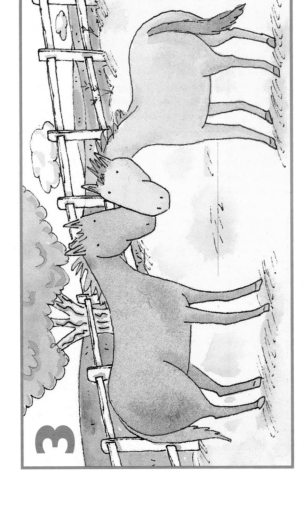

3

4

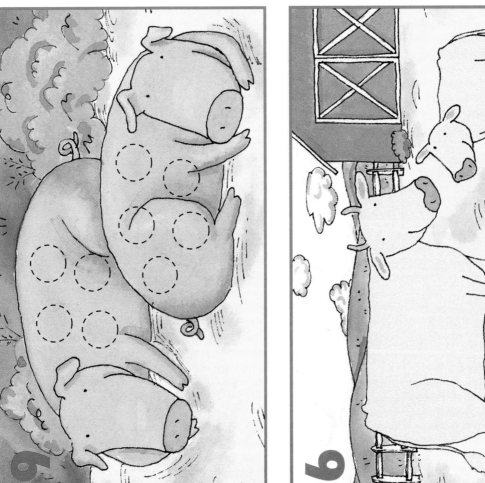

6

9

Notes for Home: Your child showed different ways to make numbers.
Home Activity: Have your child use 2 different pasta shapes to show
another way to make each number on the page.

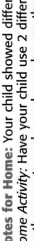

Time and Money

In the Neighborhood

TOYS

We open at

BOOKS

We open at
9:00

We open

Math at Home

Dear Family,

We will be learning about time and money. I can practice counting and using pennies, nickels, and dimes playing a game of "Fruit Stand" with you. Here's what we can do:

Put Fruit on the Table
Put a price tag next to each fruit.
First, I'll be the buyer. I'll take some pennies, nickels, and dimes. I'll count my money to buy fruit. Then we switch roles.

Community Connection

On a shopping trip or other trip through the neighborhood, play a "clock watch" game with your child. Discuss the different kinds of clocks you see and why they are where you see them.

Visit our Web site. www.parent.mathsurf.com

Discuss Before and After

Before	After

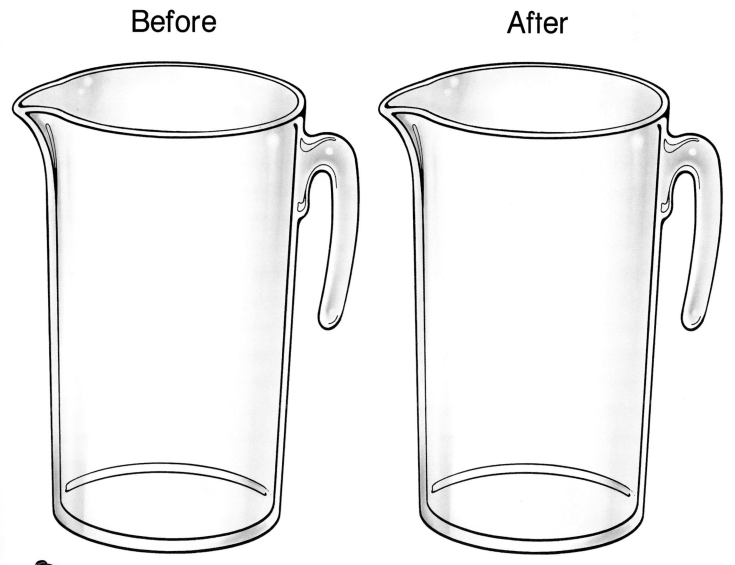

Notes for Home: Your child showed what a pitcher of water looked like before and after a powdered drink mix was added. *Home Activity:* Ask your child what an egg (or other food) looks like before and after you cook it.

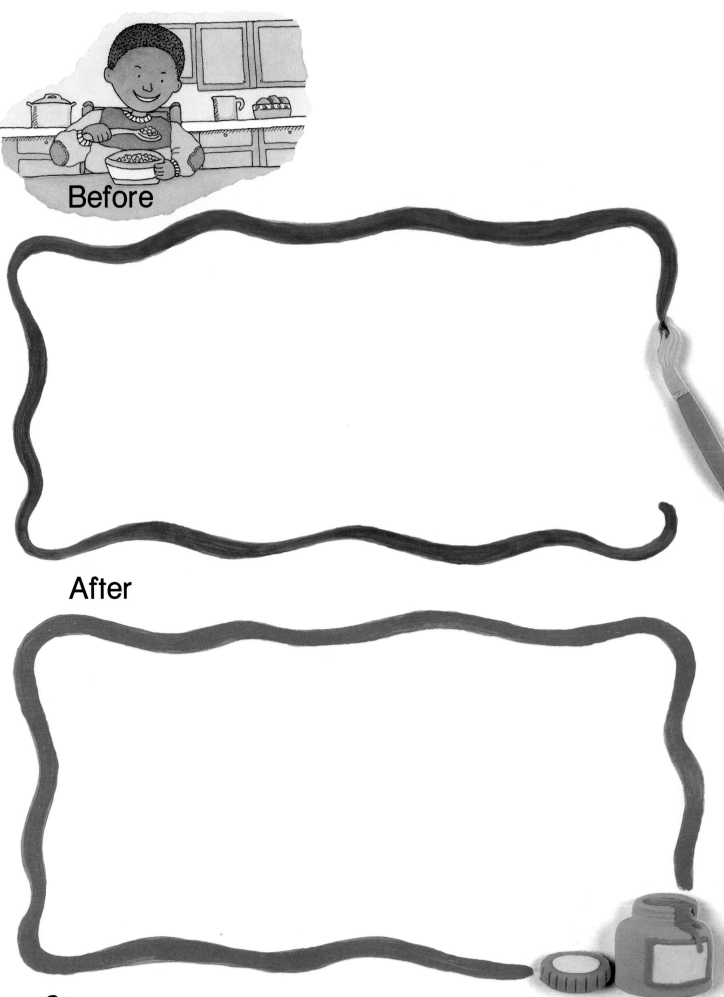

Before

After

Notes for Home: Your child drew pictures of something he or she does before school and after school.
Home Activity: Ask your child to talk about something done before dinner and something done after dinner.

Write.

Notes for Home: Your child ordered events by writing 1, 2, and 3 next to pictures to show what happened first, next, and last. *Home Activity:* Ask your child to use the words *first, next,* and *last* to describe brushing his or her teeth.

Write.

Notes for Home: Your child ordered events by describing what happened first, next, and last and writing 1, 2, and 3 next to the pictures. *Home Activity:* Ask your child to use the words *first, next,* and *last* to describe getting ready for school.

Circle.

Locate Numbers on a Clock

Notes for Home: Your child circled each clock in the pictures. *Home Activity:* Ask your child to show you three different kinds of clocks around your home.

 Notes for Home: Your child wrote the numbers on the clock. *Home Activity:* Ask your child to count from 1 to 12.

Color. Write.

Tell Time to the Hour

What time is it?

 o'clock

o'clock

4:00

6:00

 o'clock

 o'clock

 Notes for Home: Your child colored the hour on each clock and recorded the time shown.
Home Activity: Ask your child to point out analog (with hands) and digital (readout like: 9:00)
clocks in your home or neighborhood.

Color. Write.

 o'clock

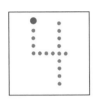

 o'clock

 o'clock

 o'clock

 o'clock

 o'clock

Notes for Home: Your child wrote the time to the hour, shown on each clock, in two ways.
Home Activity: Ask your child to read a clock, to the hour, several times throughout the day.

216 two hundred sixteen

Draw.

Problem Solving: Make a Picture

 Notes for Home: Your child drew pictures of things to do around your home. *Home Activity:* Ask your child to help you make a shopping list by drawing pictures of the items you need to buy.

Chapter 9 Lesson 5

two hundred seventeen **217**

Notes for Home: Ask your child to draw pictures to show everything needed to prepare his or her favorite cereal. *Home Activity:* If possible, help your child use the pictures to make cereal.

Name _____

Draw. Write.

| 1¢ | 2¢ | 3¢ | 4¢ | 5¢ | 6¢ | 7¢ | 8¢ | 9¢ |

☐ ¢

Notes for Home: Your child showed different amounts of money up to 9 cents.
Home Activity: Ask your child to show you a coin that is the same as 5 pennies.

Write.

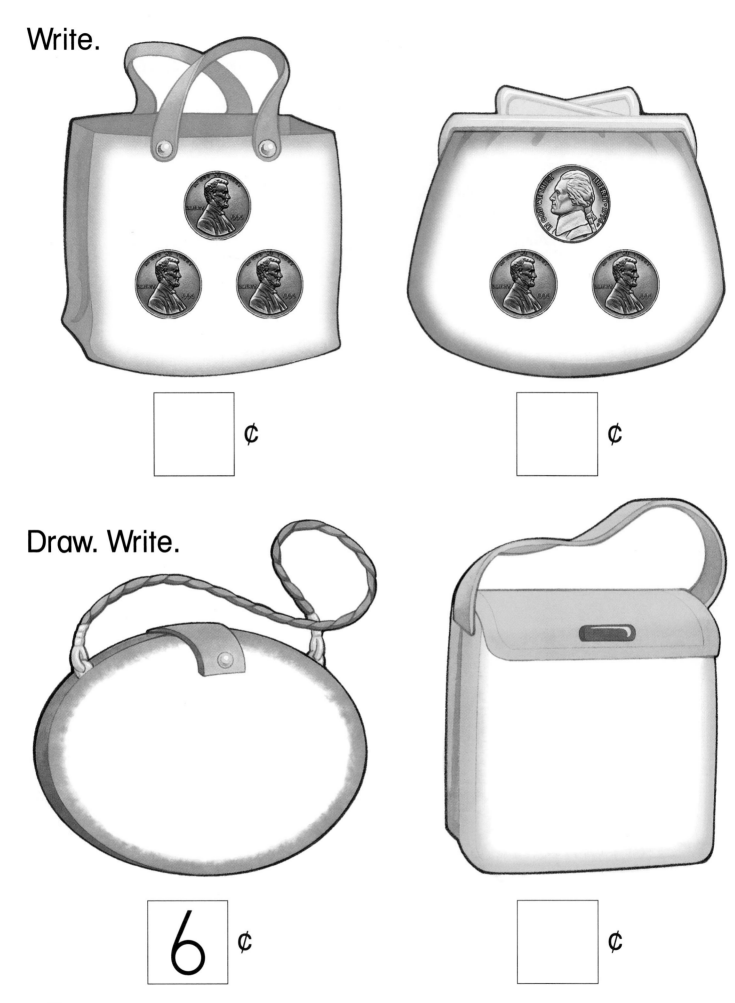

□ ¢

□ ¢

Draw. Write.

6 ¢

□ ¢

Draw. Write.

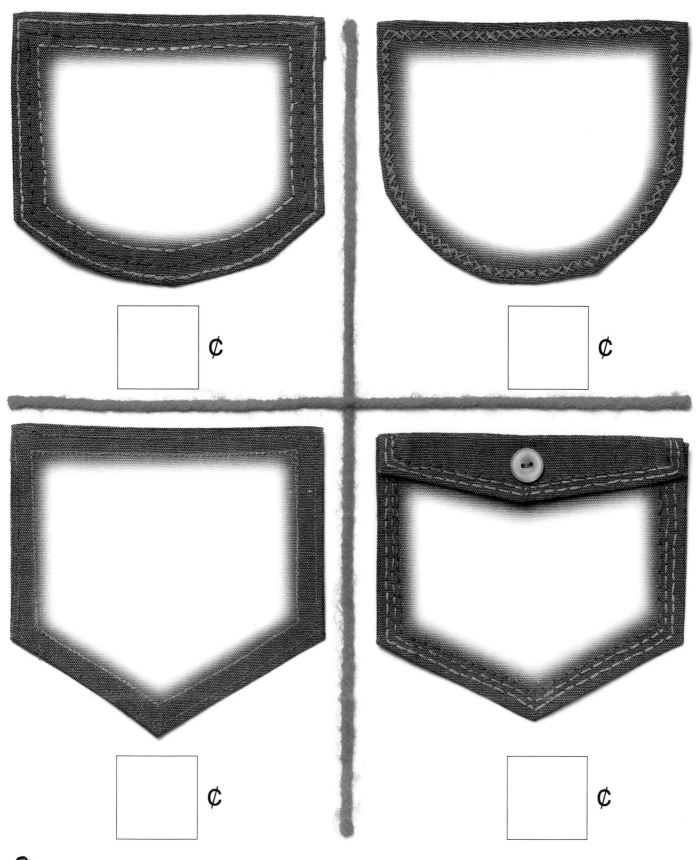

¢

¢

¢

¢

 Notes for Home: Your child put coins in each pocket, then wrote how many cents are in each.
Home Activity: Ask your child to count up to 9¢ and tell you how much money was counted.

Circle.

3¢   (7¢)   6¢   4¢   3¢   5¢

9¢   7¢   5¢   2¢   5¢   6¢

 Notes for Home: Your child circled the amount of money in each bank. *Home Activity:* Ask your child to count nickels and/or pennies up to 9¢ and tell you the amount.

Draw.

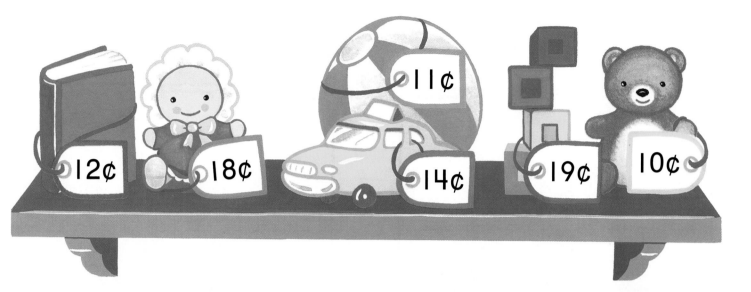

Notes for Home: Your child recorded coins needed to buy one of the toys shown.
Home Activity: Ask your child to sort dimes, nickels, and pennies and tell you how much each coin is worth.

Circle.

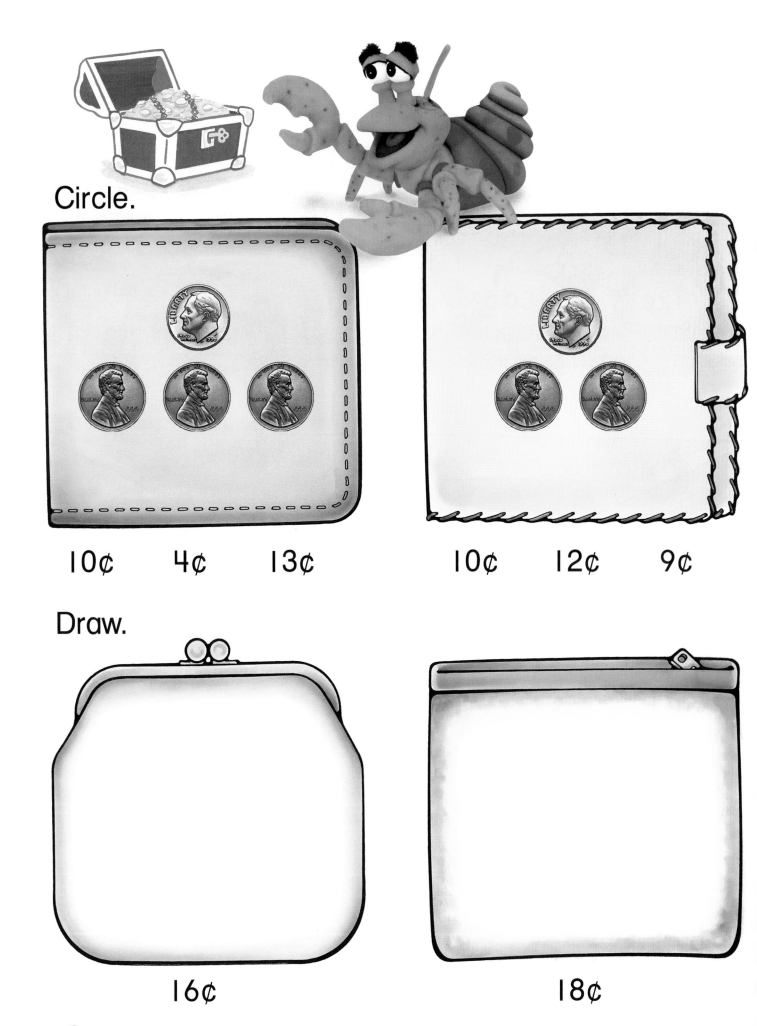

10¢   4¢   13¢   10¢   12¢   9¢

Draw.

16¢   18¢

Circle.

Draw. Write.

 Notes for Home: Your child compared prices to determine which costs more, then drew something that costs more and wrote the amount. *Home Activity:* Ask your child to point out prices when you shop together.

Circle.

Draw. Write.

 Notes for Home: Your child compared prices to determine which costs less, then drew something that costs less and wrote the amount. *Home Activity:* Ask your child to show you two different amounts of money and tell you which is more and which is less.

Name

Notes for Home: Your child talked about what happens when you go shopping and identified something the boy could buy for 10¢. *Home Activity:* Ask your child to talk about how much things cost when you shop together.

Notes for Home: Your child selected one or more fruit to buy with 19¢ and showed how much money was needed for each one. *Home Activity:* Ask your child to act out buying something at home.

228 two hundred twenty-eight

Name

Chapter 9 Review/Test

Circle.

Write.

____ : 00

_____

- - - - - - - - - - -

_____ o'clock

Write.

Notes for Home: Your child followed specific directions to show an understanding of before and after, telling time to the hour, and ordering events. *Home Activity:* Ask your child to name 3 things in order that happened during the day.

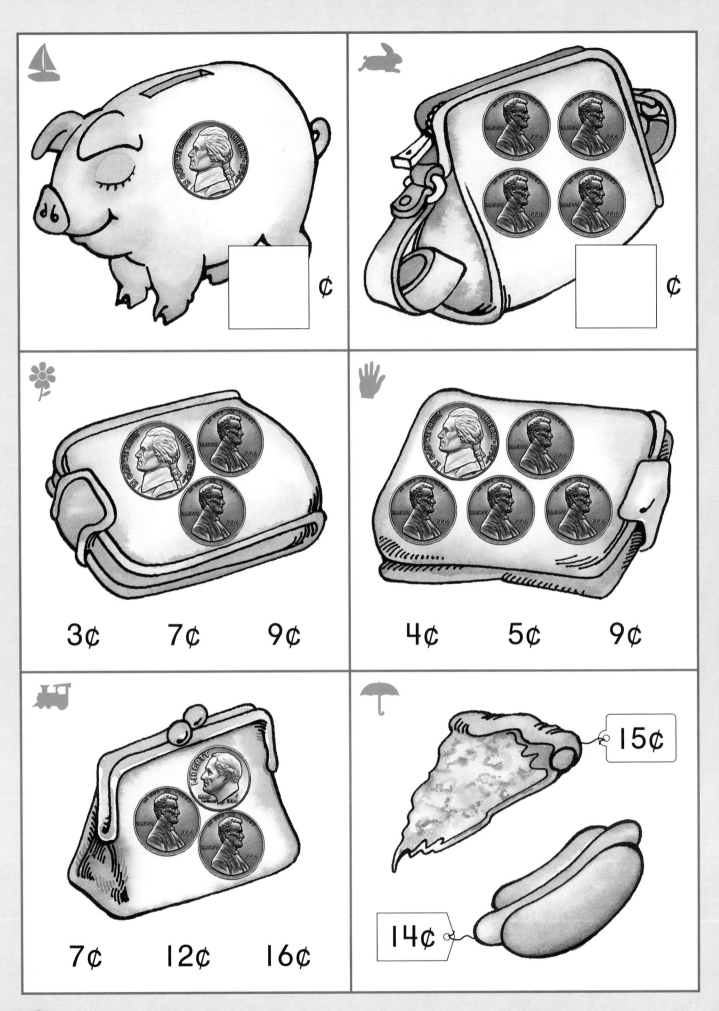

3¢   7¢   9¢

4¢   5¢   9¢

7¢   12¢   16¢

15¢

14¢

Coin Patterns

What You Need

Pencil or Crayon

Coins

Paper

What You Do

1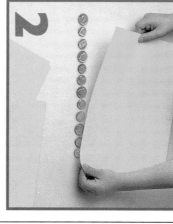

Make a pattern.

2

Put paper over coins.

3

Rub gently.

4

Show.

4

Fold down

MathSoup

Scott Foresman - Addison Wesley   My Math Magazine   No. 9

Skip Along Penny Path

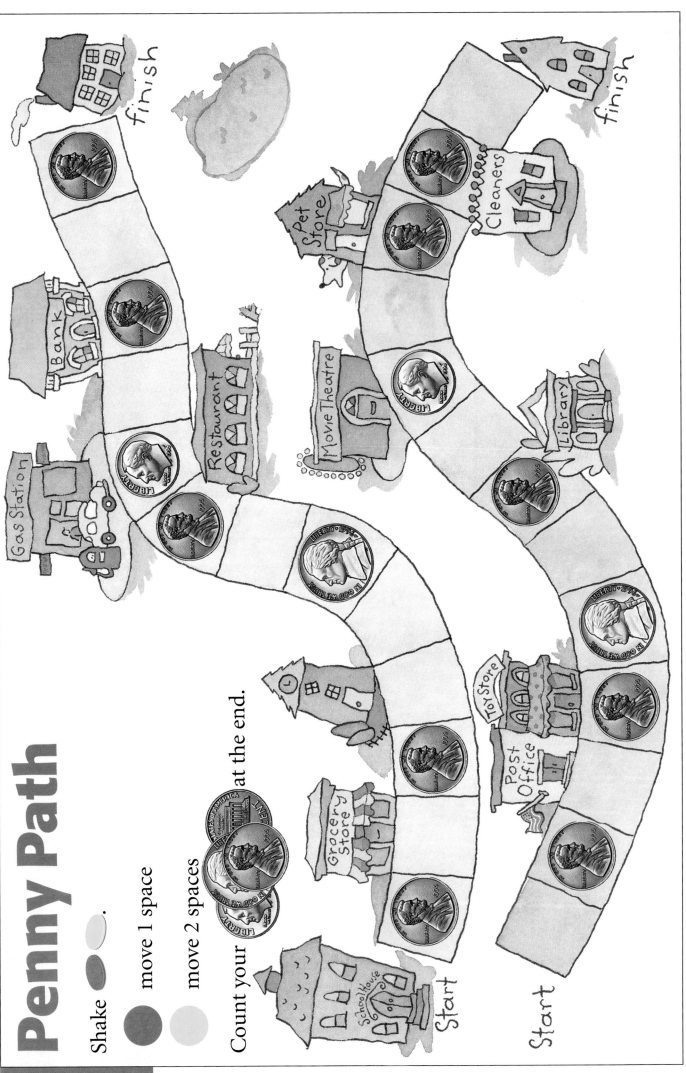

Penny Path

Shake

• move 1 space

move 2 spaces

Count your at the end.

finish

finish

Start

Start

Schoolhouse

Grocery Store

Toy Store

Post Office

Library

Movie Theatre

Pet Store

Cleaners

Restaurant

Gas Station

Bank

🎒 **Notes for Home:** Your child played this game with a partner.
Home Activity: Ask your child to play the game with you. You will
need 2 buttons or other markers, 2 dimes, 2 nickels, and 9 pennies.

Wonderful Water

Fish Chow

Notes for Home: Your child used the picture to talk about joining, separating, and comparing groups.
Home Activity: Ask your child to make two groups of towels, count how many in each group, and tell how many in both groups.

Math at Home

Dear Family,

We will be learning about joining, separating, and comparing groups. I can practice what I've learned by helping to wash the dishes. Here's what we can do:

Clear the Table

1. Ask me to bring 2 dishes to the sink.
2. Then ask me to bring 3 more dishes.
3. We'll count and tell how many dishes in the sink all together.
4. We can repeat with different combinations until the table is clear.

Community Connection

Help your child tell "joining" or "separating" stories about things you see in your neighborhood. For example: There were 2 people at the bus stop. Then 2 more people came. Now there are 4 people.

💻≈💻 **Visit our Web site.** www.parent.mathsurf.com

Explore Joining

Notes for Home: Your child told stories about joining groups. *Home Activity:* Ask your child to point out two groups of spoons or other items and make up a joining story about them.

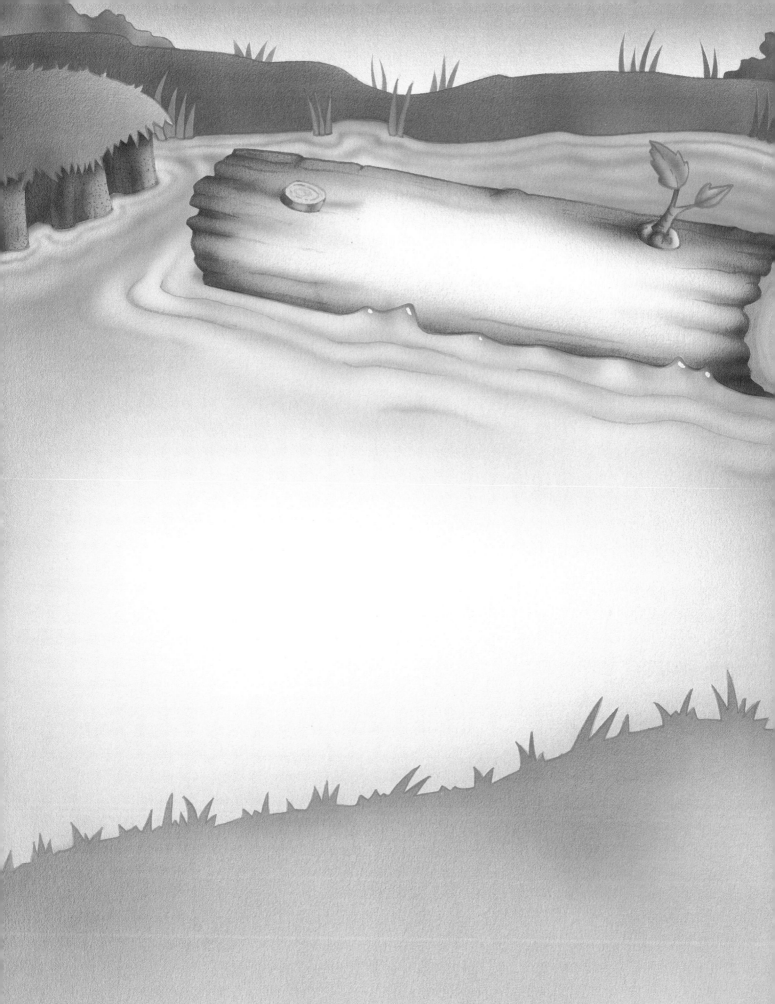

Notes for Home: Your child used cubes to tell joining stories about two groups of frogs.
Home Activity: Ask your child to use pennies to tell a joining story about two groups of frogs.

Name _____

3   2

[ ]

Write. Draw.

[ ]   [ ]

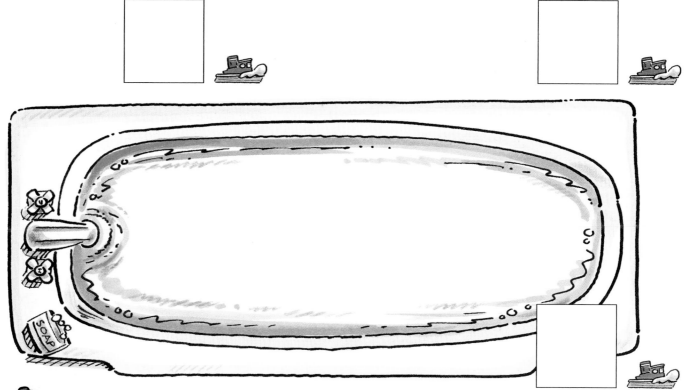

[ ]

Notes for Home: Your child built Snap Cube tugboat trains, then told stories about joining groups.
Home Activity: Ask your child to make two groups from 5 small objects and then tell a joining story about the groups.

Write. Draw.

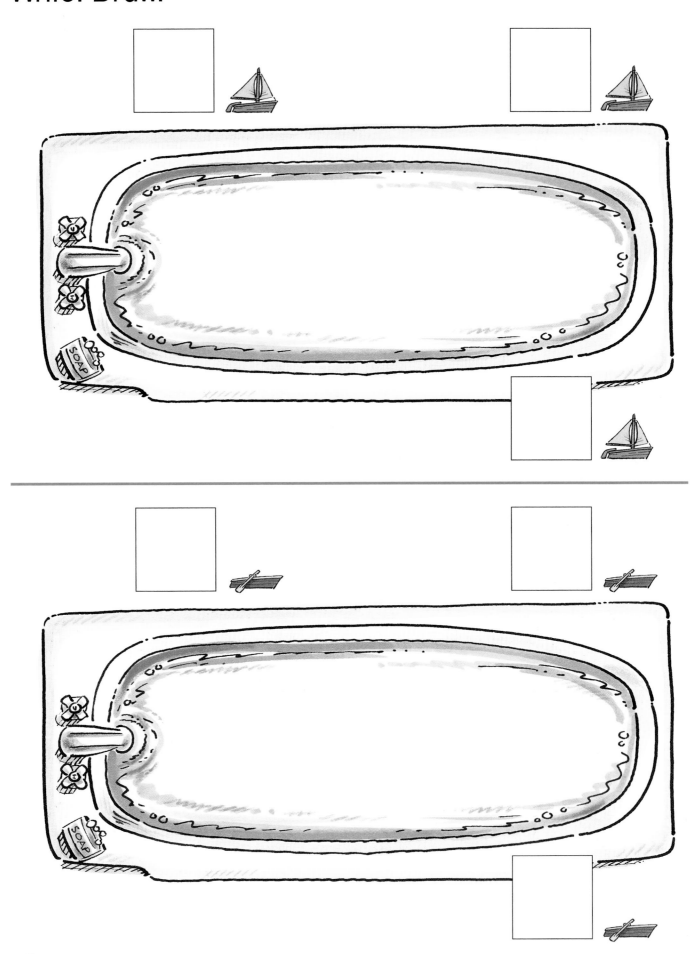

Explore Separating

Circle.

Notes for Home: Your child listened to and told stories about separating groups, then told how many were left. *Home Activity:* Ask your child to tell a story about separating groups of clothes. For example: I have 4 shirts. We put 2 in the drawer. How many shirts are left?

Chapter 10 Lesson 3   two hundred thirty-nine **239**

Draw.

Notes for Home: Your child told stories about separating groups, used counters to act them out, and then recorded one. *Home Activity:* Ask your child to use small objects such as pennies to act out a story about separating groups.

240   two hundred forty

Separate Groups and Lengths

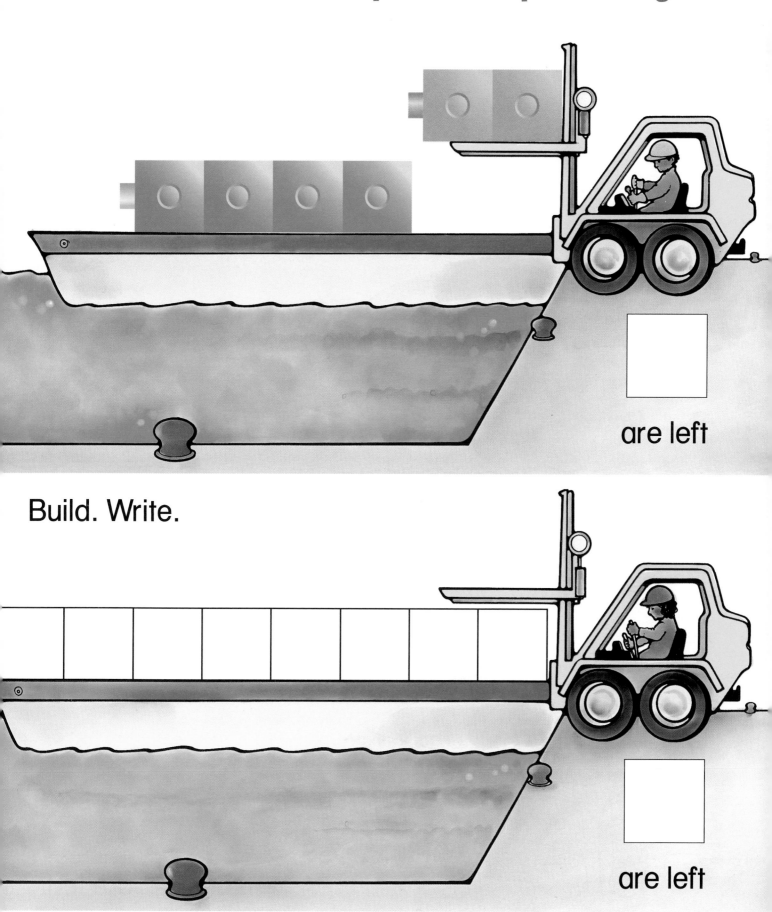

are left

Build. Write.

are left

Notes for Home: Your child listened to and told stories about separating groups and used Snap Cubes to record what happened. *Home Activity:* Ask your child to place pennies on the cargo boat and then tell stories about separating groups by unloading it.

Build. Write.

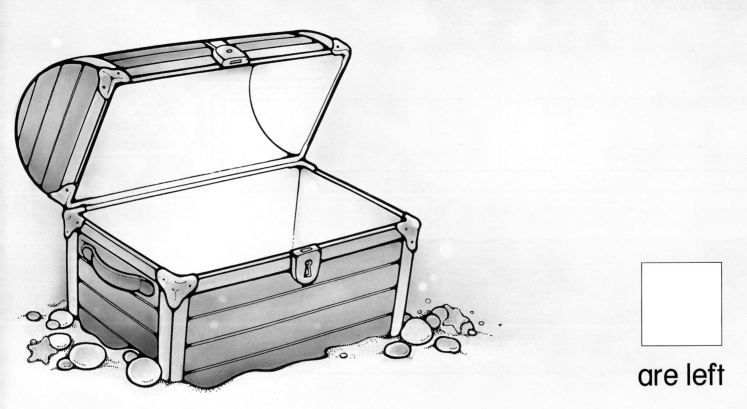

☐ **are left**

☐ **are left**

 Notes for Home: Your child used Snap Cubes to show separating stories in each scene and then wrote the number to tell how many were left. *Home Activity:* Ask your child to use fingers to act out a story about separating groups.

242   two hundred forty-two

Name

Notes for Home: Your child drew people to show joining or separating groups. *Home Activity:* Ask your child to use pennies to show two groups and then tell a joining or separating story about them.

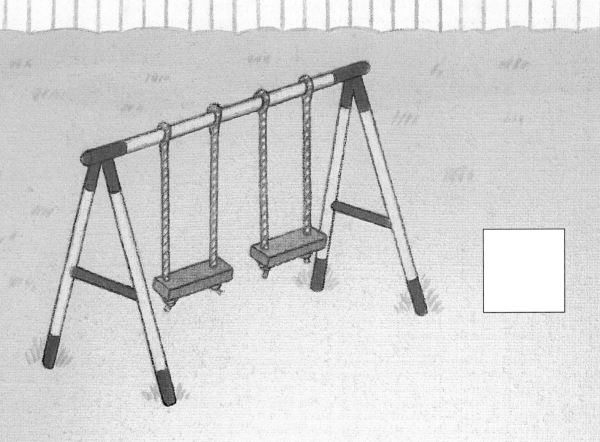

Name _____

Draw. Compare.

 Notes for Home: Your child used counters to record groups, then circled groups to compare amounts.
Home Activity: Ask your child to use the words *more* and *fewer* to compare 2 groups of objects such as pencils or pens.

Draw more.

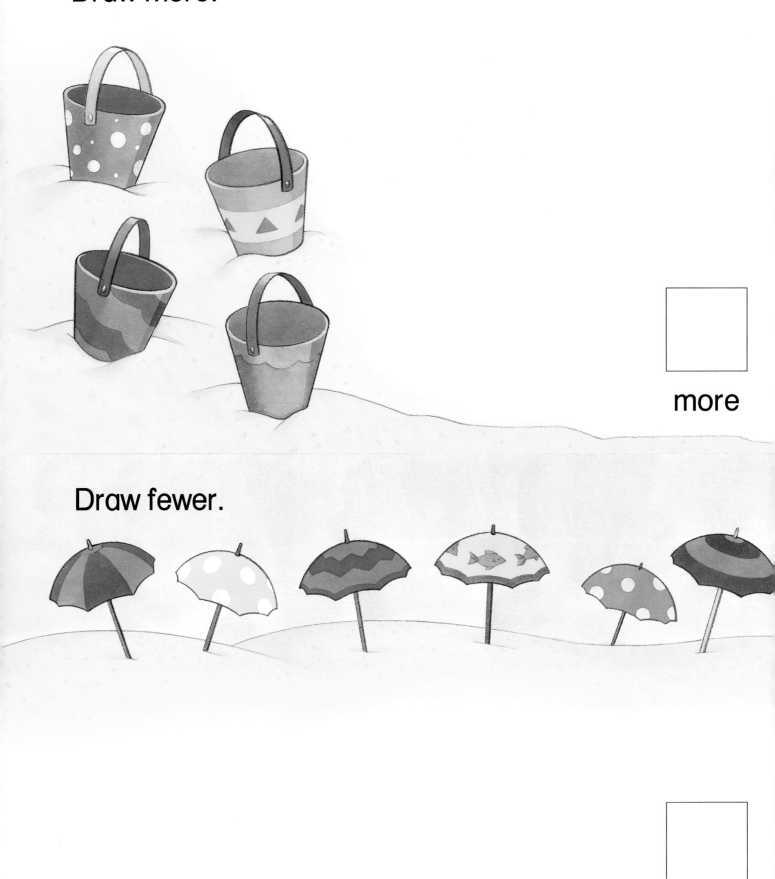

more

Draw fewer.

fewer

 Notes for Home: Your child drew a group that was more and one that was fewer and wrote numbers to tell how many. *Home Activity:* Show your child 2 groups of small objects such as pennies, and let your child tell which has more and which has fewer.

Compare Groups and Lengths

Compare. Color.

Build.

Notes for Home: Your child compared the top 2 fish and colored the longer one yellow; drew Snap Cube trains longer or shorter than the bottom fish. *Home Activity:* Ask your child to use the words *longer* and *shorter* to compare 2 objects such as pencils.

Chapter 10 Lesson 7   two hundred forty-seven   247

Compare. Color. Write.

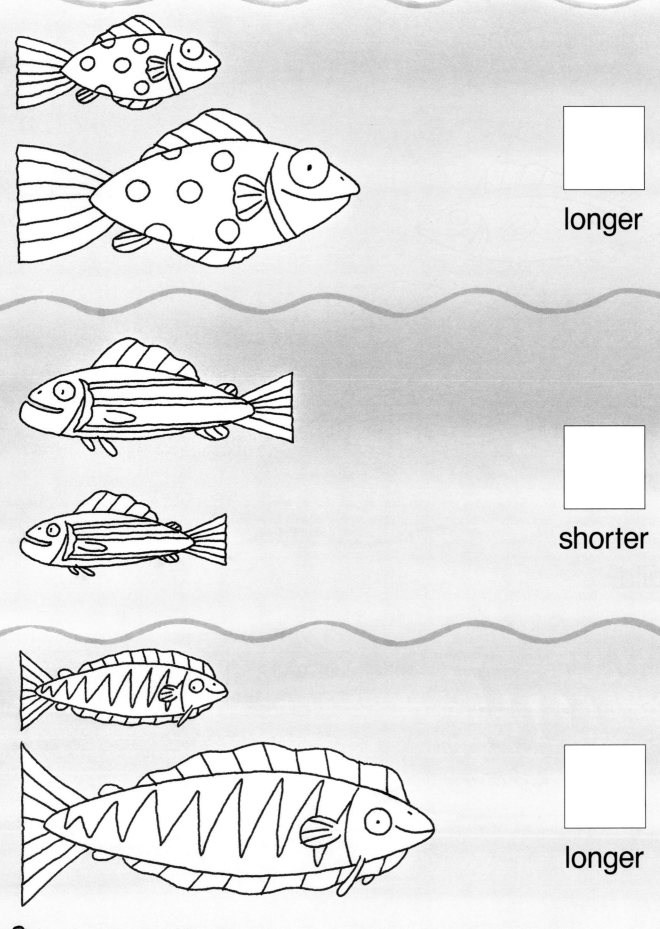

longer

shorter

longer

 Notes for Home: For each pair, your child colored the longer fish yellow, compared their lengths with Snap Cubes, and wrote numbers to tell how many longer or shorter. *Home Activity:* Ask your child to build and compare two chains of paper clips, telling how many more clips in the longer chain.

Problem Solving: Use Logical Reasoning

Circle.

Notes for Home: Your child listened to a story and used logical reasoning to identify each answer.
Home Activity: Ask your child to use logical reasoning to solve problems at home, for example:
How many more plates do we need to finish setting the table?

Draw.

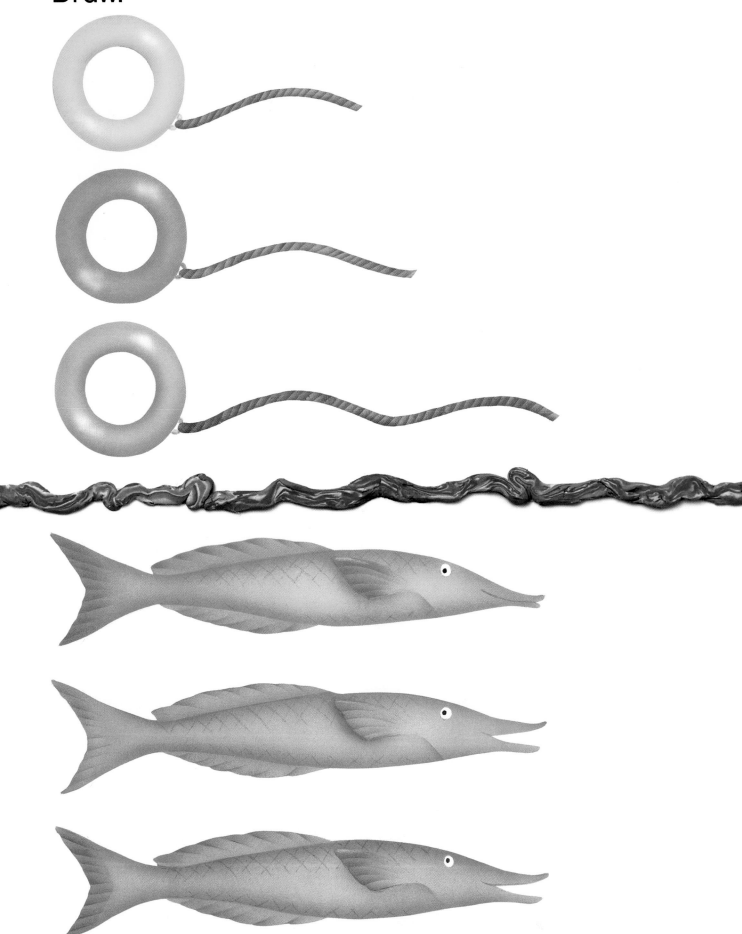

 Notes for Home: Your child identified each answer and then drew pictures. *Home Activity:* Ask your child to use logical reasoning to solve problems at home, for example: I need a large red cup. I have a small blue cup, a small red cup, and a large yellow cup. Do I have the one I need?

250 two hundred fifty

Chapter 10 Review/Test

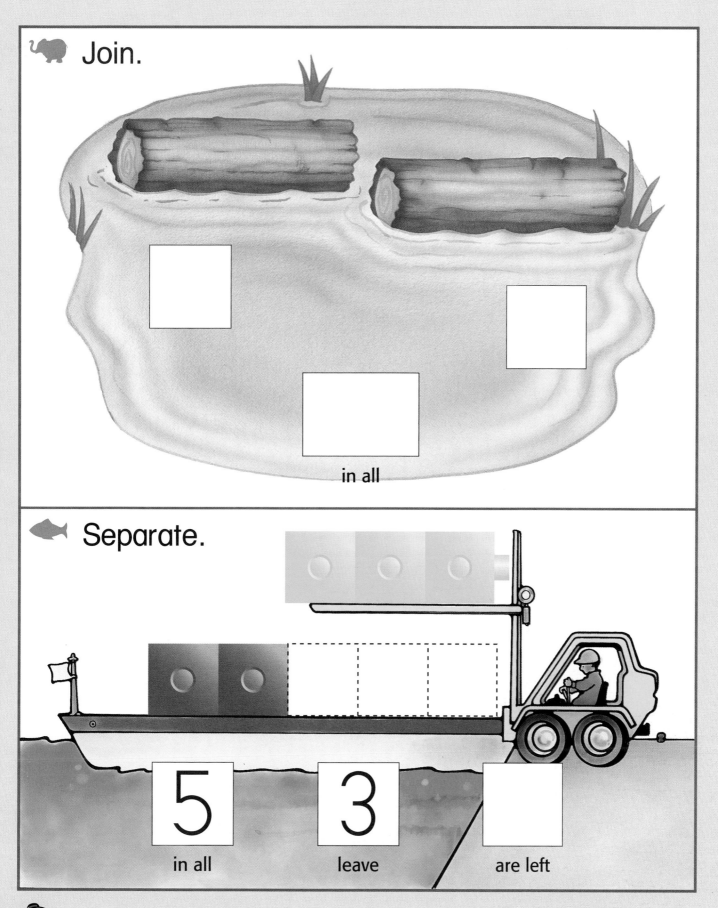

Join.

in all

Separate.

5	3	
in all	leave	are left

Notes for Home: Your child joined and separated groups, then wrote the number to show how many in all or how many are left. *Home Activity:* Ask your child to make two groups of snack foods and tell a joining story and a separating story about them.

Draw more.

 Draw fewer.

 Color. Write.

 Notes for Home: Your child compared groups and lengths, then wrote how many more.
Home Activity: Show your child two groups of objects, and ask him or her to use the words *more* and *fewer* to talk about them.

Fish Tales

What You Need

Paper
Crayons
Scissors
Tape

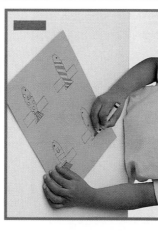

What You Do

1

Make fish finger puppets.

Cut.

3

Tape.

4

Make your own fish tales.

Fold down

MathSoup

Scott Foresman - Addison Wesley   My Math Magazine   No. 10

Fishy Friends

Tugboat Fun

Players 1 or more

What You Need

1 card for each color

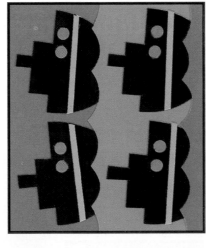

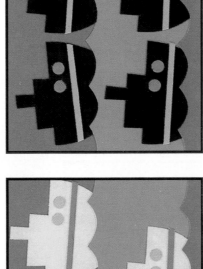

What You Do

Each player picks 2 cards.

Find the tugboats that match the colors.

Count how many tugboats in all.

Take turns.

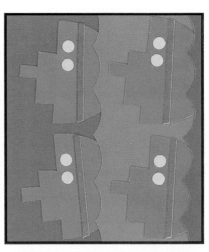

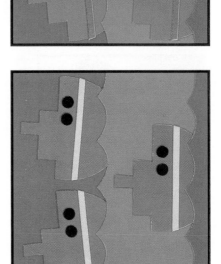

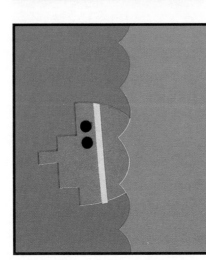
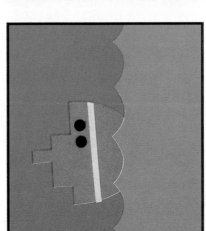

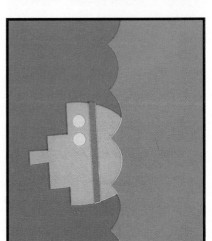

Notes for Home: Your child played a game to practice joining groups.
Home Activity: Play the game with your child.

2

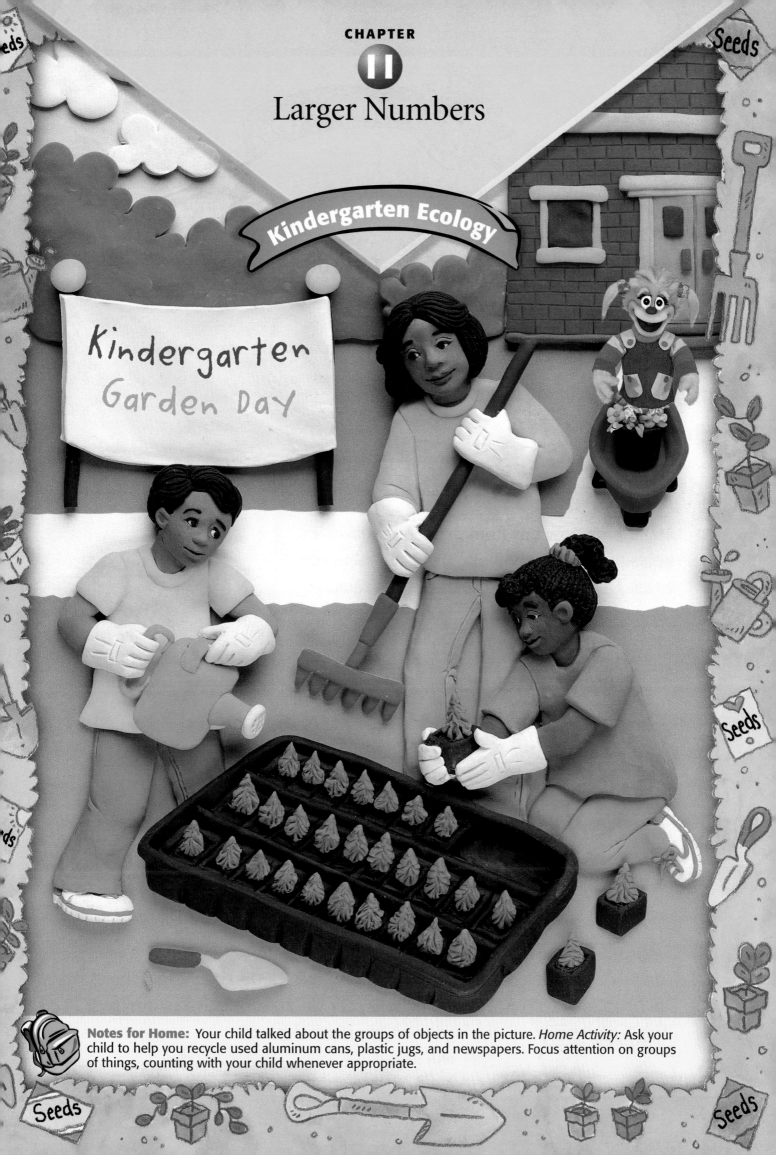

Kindergarten Ecology

Kindergarten
Garden Day

Seeds

Seeds

Seeds

Seeds

Seeds

Math at Home

Dear Family,

We will be learning how to count, write, and use larger numbers. I can practice counting by helping you plant a window garden. Here's how:

Plant a Garden

Make a window box from margarine tubs with holes punched in the bottoms. Place them on a tray. Decide what to grow. Get the seeds. Count how many will fit. We can plant them together. We will give the plants enough water and light to grow.

Community Connection Help your child make a "Pick Up Litter" sign. Then take a walk and help your child get permission and post the sign in an appropriate place.

 Visit our Web site. www.parent.mathsurf.com

Explore Numbers to 31

Circle . Color.

Draw.

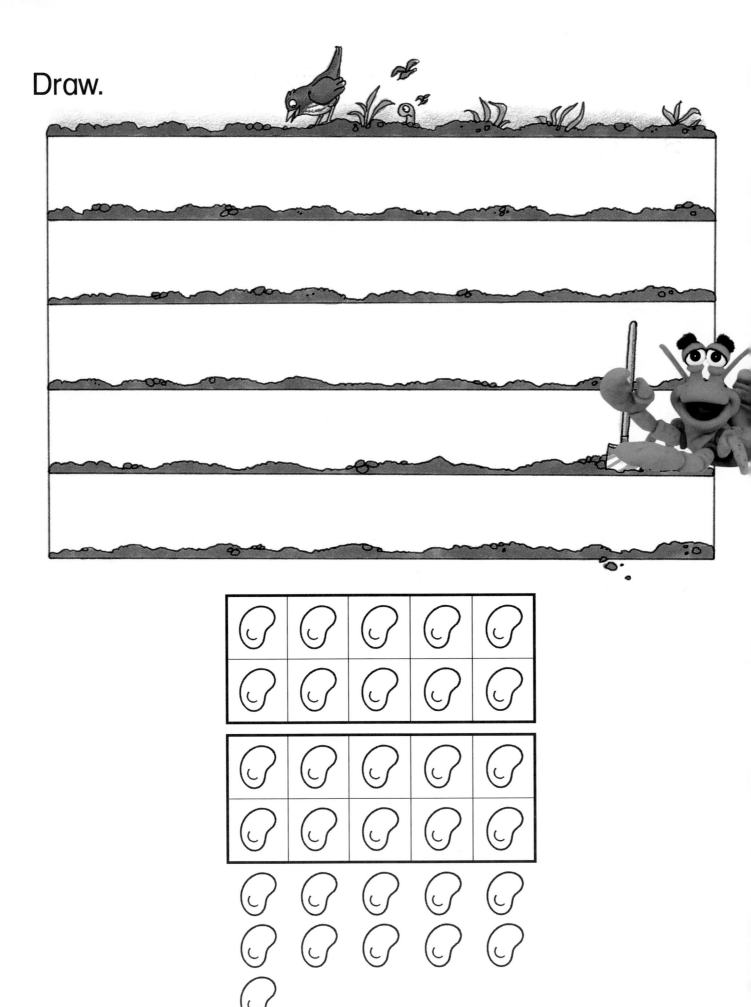

Notes for Home: Your child arranged and drew a group of beans in the garden and colored that many in and outside of the ten-frames. *Home Activity:* Ask your child to put 25 snacks into plastic bags as 10s and extras.

258   two hundred fifty-eight

Count and Write 11 to 15

Color extras. Write.

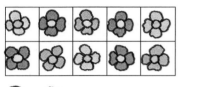

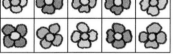

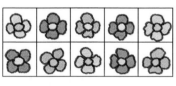

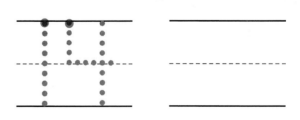

Notes for Home: Your child counted flowers, colored those outside ten-frames, and then wrote the numbers 11–15. *Home Activity:* Ask your child to show you 11 to 15 toothpicks as a group of 10 and extras.

Draw 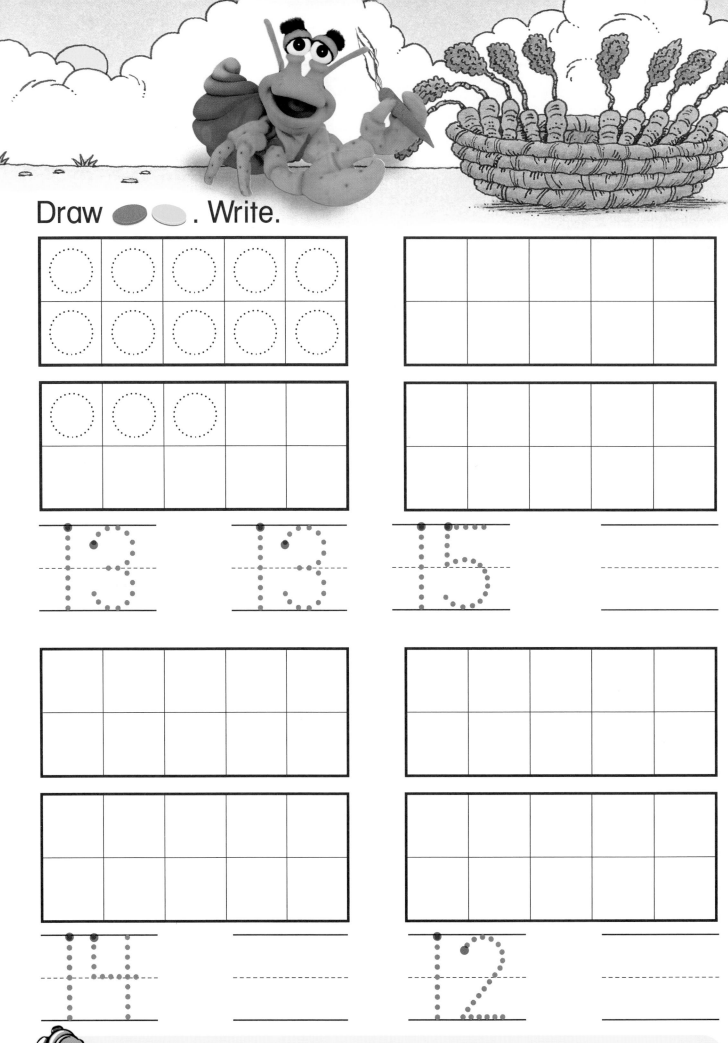. Write.

13   13   15   _____

14   _____   12   _____

Notes for Home: Your child drew circles in the ten-frames and wrote the numbers.
Home Activity: Ask your child to count groups of 11 to 15 objects.

260   two hundred sixty

Count and Write 16 to 19

Draw 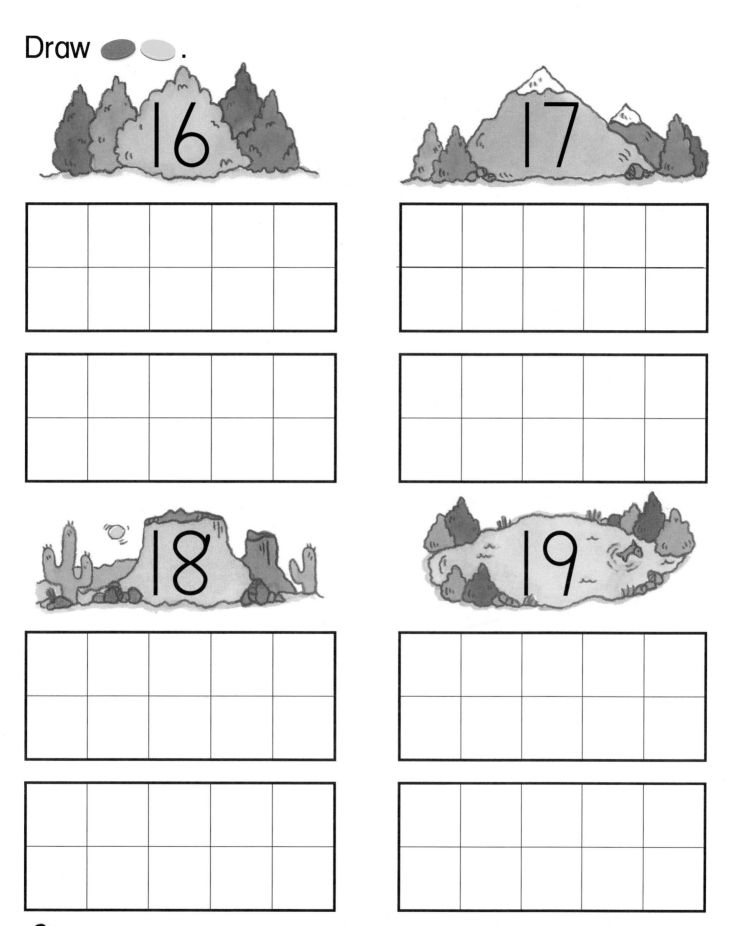.

Notes for Home: Your child drew counters in the ten-frames to show the numbers 16 through 19.
Home Activity: Ask your child to find 16 to 19 objects at home.

Chapter 11 Lesson 3   two hundred sixty-one **261**

Circle 10. Count and Write.

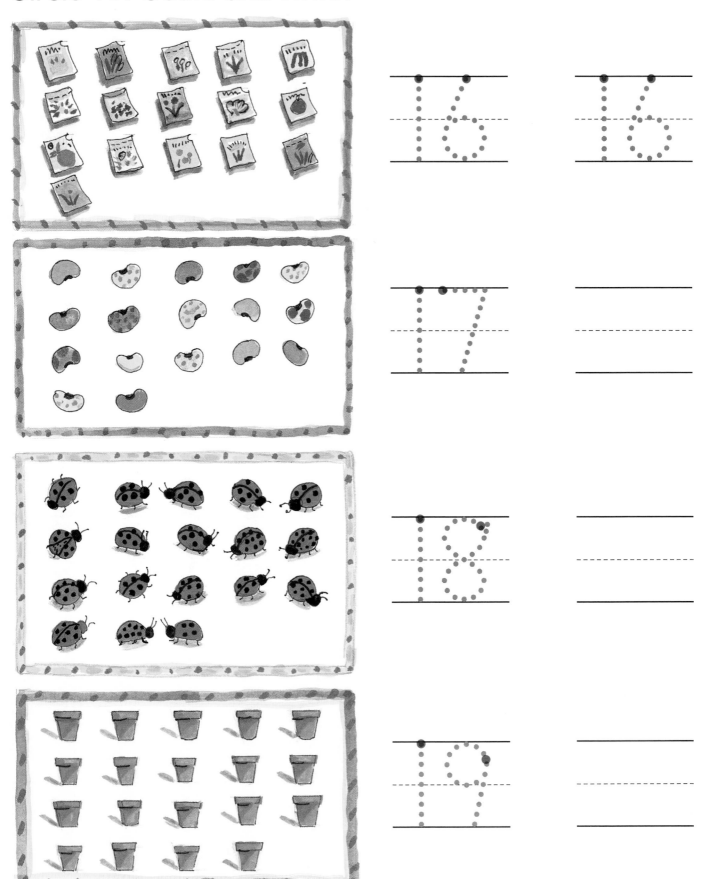

Notes for Home: Your child circled ten, counted objects, and wrote the numbers 16 through 19.
Home Activity: Ask your child to show you a group of 16 pennies as one ten and 6 extras.

262 two hundred sixty-two

Name _____

Write.

Estimate ▢

Count ▢

 Notes for Home: Your child estimated the number of beans in a bag, then drew the actual amount.
Home Activity: Ask your child to guess and count how many teaspoons are in your kitchen drawer.

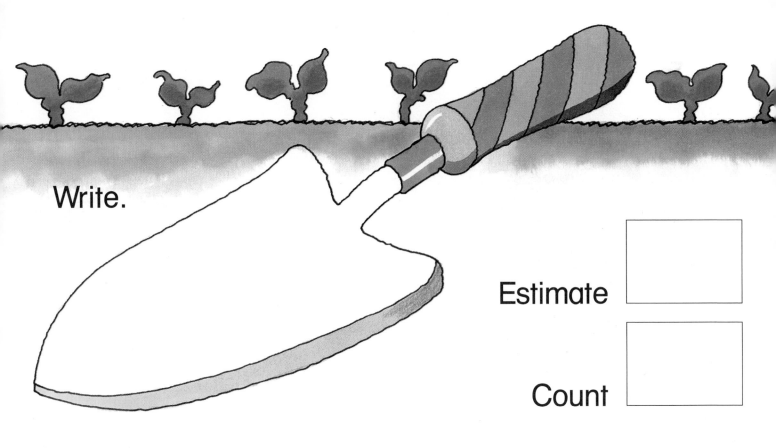

Write.

Estimate

Count

Lima Beans

Estimate

Count

Notes for Home: Your child estimated and counted to check the number of beans that fit on the trowel and seed packet. *Home Activity:* Hold 30 or fewer buttons or dry beans in your hand, and ask your child to estimate and then count how many.

Name _____

Count and Write Larger Numbers

Count. Write.

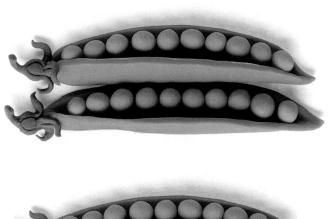

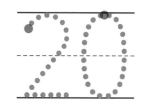

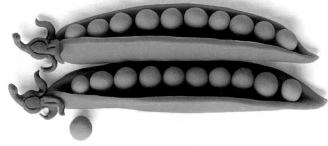

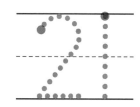

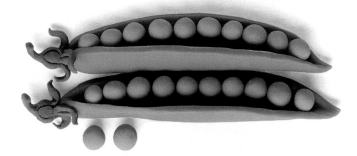

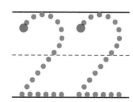

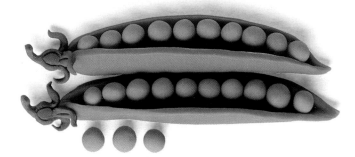

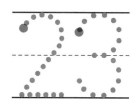

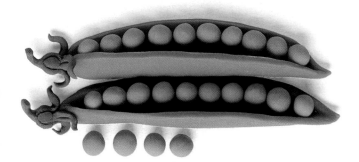

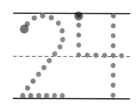

Notes for Home: Your child counted peas and wrote the numbers 20 through 24.
Home Activity: Ask your child to draw a picture of 20 things. Then talk about the different
ways to organize 20: 2 groups of 10, 4 groups of 5, and so on.

Chapter 11 Lesson 5   two hundred sixty-five **265**

Count. Write.

25

 Notes for Home: Your child counted beans and wrote the numbers 25 through 30.
Home Activity: Ask your child to draw a picture of 30 things. Talk about the different ways
to organize 30: 3 groups of 10, 6 groups of 5, and so on.

266   two hundred sixty-six

Use a Calendar

May

Sunday	Monday	Tuesday	Wednesday	Thursday	Friday	Saturday
					1	2
3	4	5	6	7	8	9
10	11	12	13	14	15	16
17	18	19	20	21	22	23
24	25	26	27	28	29	30
31						

Notes for Home: Your child practiced writing the numbers 1 to 31 on a calendar and circled special dates. *Home Activity:* Ask your child to count aloud from 1 to 31.

	Sunday	Monday	Tuesday	Wednesday	Thursday	Friday	Saturday

 Notes for Home: Show your child a calendar page for the current month and help him or her write the name of the month, write the dates, and draw a picture at the top of the page. *Home Activity:* Ask your child to help you mark any family birthdays or special events on this calendar.

Name _____

Color the box that has more.

Draw more.

Notes for Home: Your child colored the box of peaches that has more, then drew apples so the tree on the right has more. *Home Activity:* Give your child a bag with 30 cereal bits, and ask him or her to make 2 unequal groups, identifying which has more.

Circle the group that has fewer.

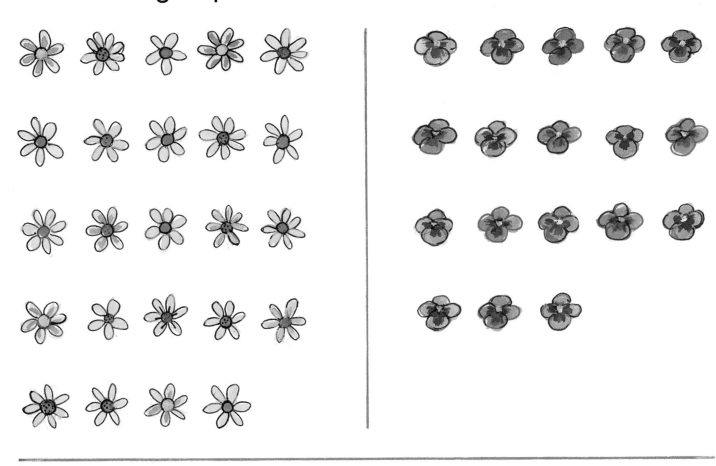

Draw fewer.

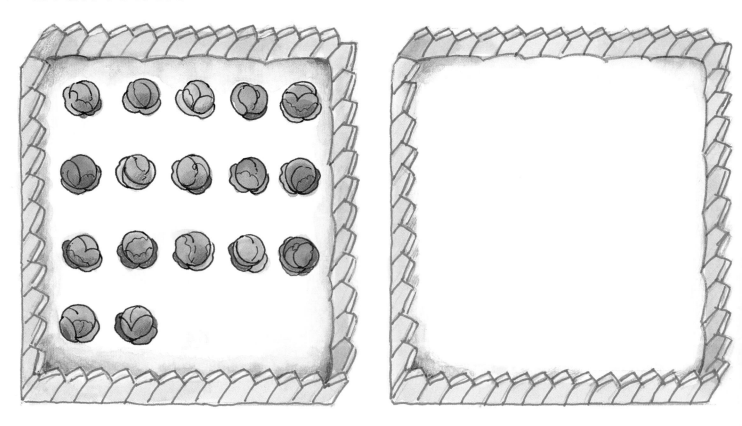

Notes for Home: Your child circled the group that has fewer. At the bottom he or she drew a group with fewer. *Home Activity:* Ask your child to compare two groups of pennies by stacking them and comparing their heights.

Use Larger Numbers for Measurement

Write.

Estimate: about

Measure: about

Estimate: about

Measure: about

 Notes for Home: Your child estimated the length of classroom objects and measured them with Snap Cubes. *Home Activity:* Ask your child to measure the width of your kitchen sink with paper clips.

Write.

Estimate: about

Measure: about

Estimate: about

Measure: about

Notes for Home: Your child estimated and measured the capacity of pots with a trowel.
Home Activity: Ask your child to estimate and then fill a bowl with spoonfuls of rice.

Name _____

Draw. Write.

about [ ] about [ ]

about [ ] about [ ]

Notes for Home: Your child drew and measured the length of classroom objects with paper clips and straws. *Home Activity:* Help your child measure the length of a couch with straws and paper clips, or other available items that can be used as units of measure.

Circle.

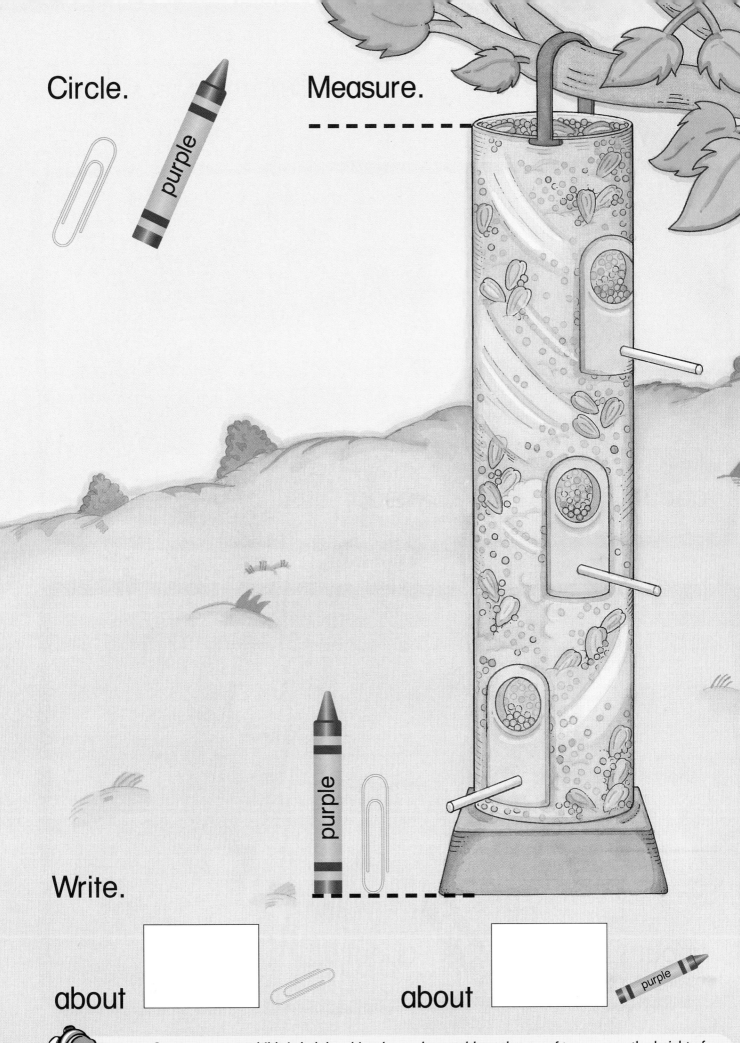

Measure.

Write.

about [ ]

about [ ]

Notes for Home: Your child circled the object he or she would need more of to measure the height of the bird feeder. Then he or she used both paperclips and crayons to measure and wrote how many.
Home Activity: Ask your child to measure the length of his or her bed, each time using different shoes.

Chapter 11 Review/Test

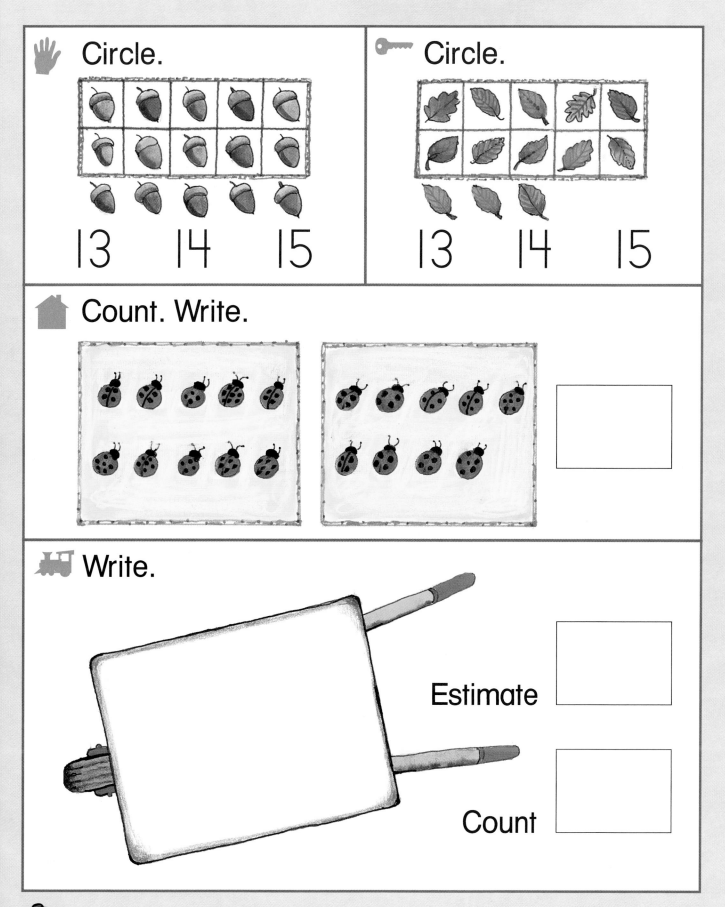

Circle.

13   14   15

Circle.

13   14   15

Count. Write.

Write.

Estimate

Count

Notes for Home: Your child wrote or circled numbers to show an understanding of numbers larger than 10. *Home Activity:* Ask your child to assemble a group of 18 objects—pennies, toothpicks, cereal pieces, and so on.

Estimate.

Measure.

February

Sunday	Monday	Tuesday	Wednesday	Thursday	Friday	Saturday
1	2					
	9					14
15						
22						

Notes for Home: Your child counted, measured, and wrote numbers up to 31. *Home Activity:* Ask your child to count to 31 on a July calendar.

Trash Sculpture

What You Need

Small Metal and Plastic Objects
Cardboard Tubes
Egg Carton
Paper Cups or Plates
Tape and Glue
Box Lid

What You Do

Get materials.

1

Tape or glue.

2

Show.

3

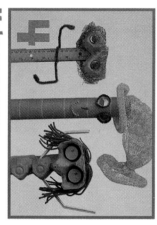

Make some more.

4

Fold down

MathSurf

Scott Foresman - Addison Wesley   My Math Magazine   No. 11

Terrific Trash

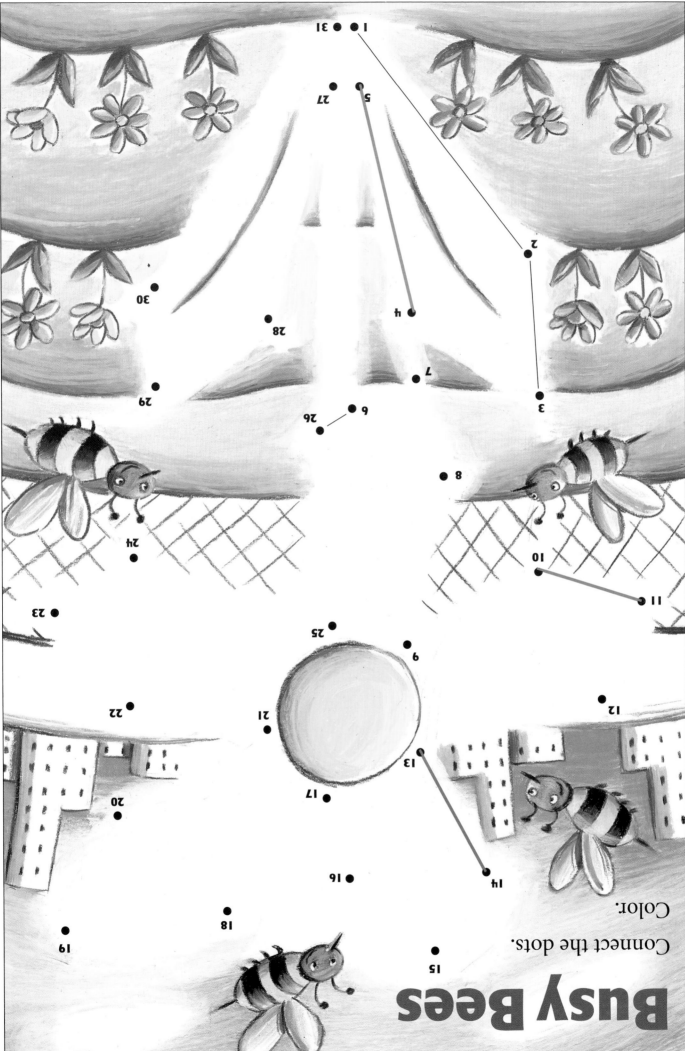

Busy Bees

Connect the dots.
Color.

Notes for Home: Your child connected the dots from 1 to 31 in order to discover an object in the garden. *Home Activity:* Ask your child to count aloud from 1 to 31.

World of Animals

Notes for Home: Your child talked about the groups in the picture. *Home Activity:* Ask your child to point to animals that are joining other animals.

Math at Home

Dear Family,

We will be learning about adding and subtracting. I can practice what I've learned by telling stories about animals. Here is what we can do:

Dog Stories

Let's get 10 buttons or pennies and pretend they are dogs. Let's pretend a plastic container is a doghouse. You put 4 "dogs" in the dog house. I add 1 more "dog" and tell how many in all. You can put 6 "dogs" in the dog house. I can take 2 "dogs" away and tell how many are left. We can use different numbers and tell other dog stories.

Community Connection

When you walk through your neighborhood with your child, look for examples of addition or subtraction stories. For example: There are 4 cars parked on the street. One car drives away. How many are left?

Visit our Web site. www.parent.mathsurf.com

Sums to 5

Circle.

Draw.

Write.

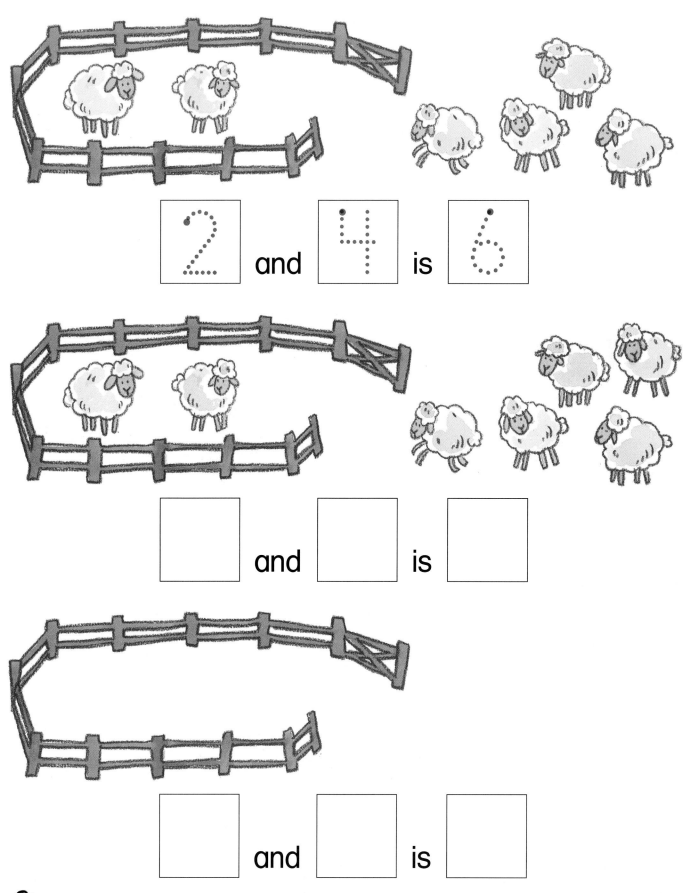

2 and 4 is 6

[ ] and [ ] is [ ]

[ ] and [ ] is [ ]

Notes for Home: Your child wrote the numbers to tell an addition story for each picture.
Home Activity: Ask your child to use stuffed animals or toys to act out adding a number to 1.

Draw. Write.

3 and 2 is 5

3 and 4 is ☐

2 and 4 is ☐

3 and 2 is ☐

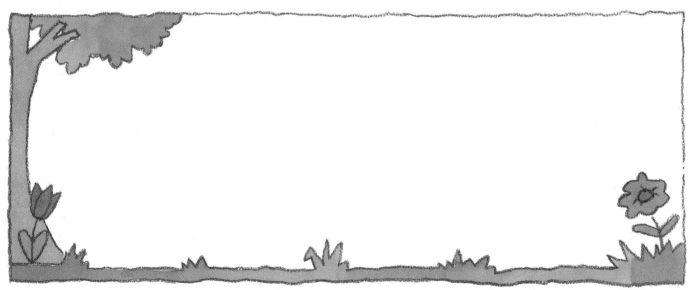

Notes for Home: Your child wrote the sums for the joining actions. *Home Activity:* Ask your child to act out adding 1, 2, or 3 using stuffed animals.

284 two hundred eighty-four

Sums to 8 and 9

Use ⬤ ⬤ .
Draw 🦴. Write.

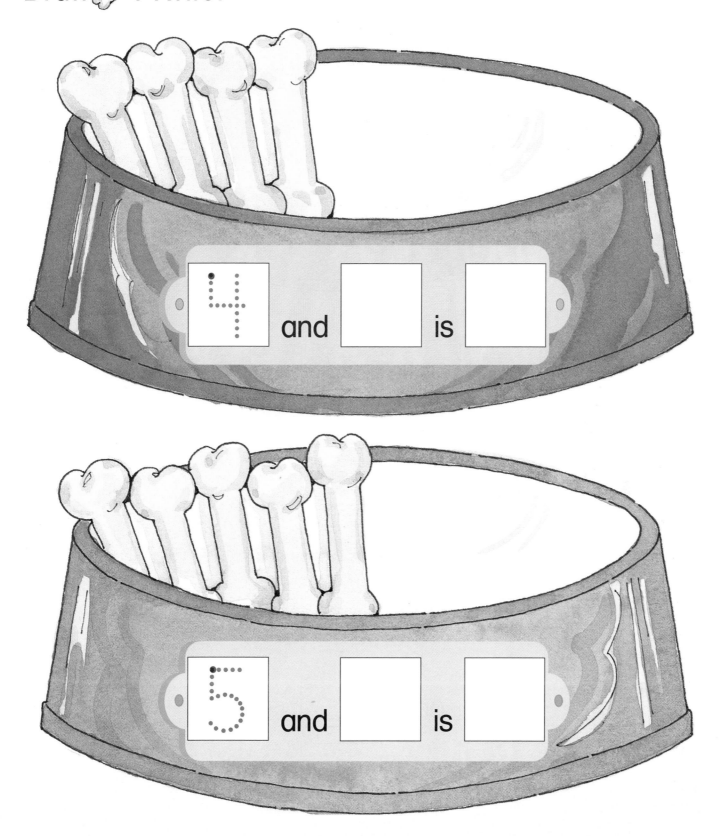

4 and ☐ is ☐

5 and ☐ is ☐

Notes for Home: Your child recorded two number stories about joining groups of 4 and 5 dog biscuits.
Home Activity: Ask your child to tell a story about 4 animals in a tree joined by 4 or 5 more.

Use . Write.

1 and 7 is 8

5 and 2 is ☐

4 and 4 is ☐

5 and 1 is ☐

2 and 7 is ☐

 Notes for Home: Your child used counters to join the groups, then wrote the sum.
Home Activity: Ask your child to use snack foods to show 3 and 6.

$$5 + 5 = 10$$

Draw. Write.

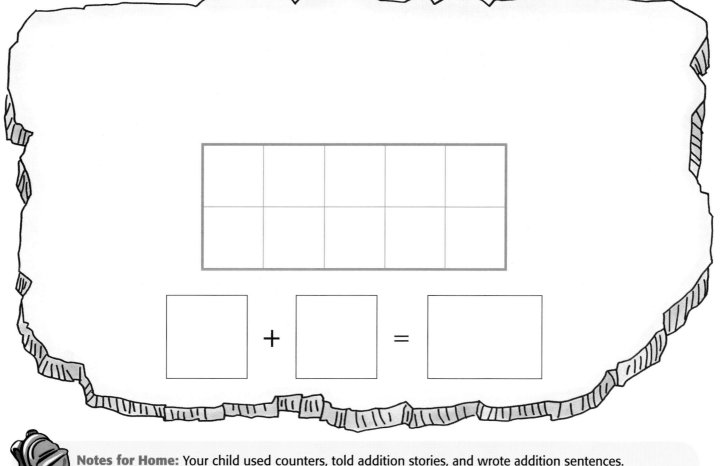

$$\boxed{} + \boxed{} = \boxed{}$$

Notes for Home: Your child used counters, told addition stories, and wrote addition sentences.
Home Activity: Ask your child to use 10 small objects such as buttons to act out a number story.

Color. Write.

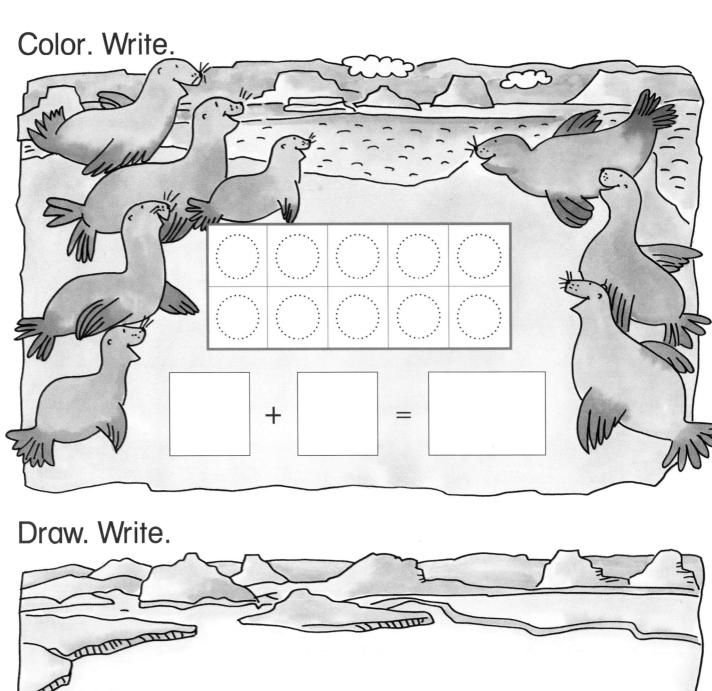

☐ + ☐ = ☐

Draw. Write.

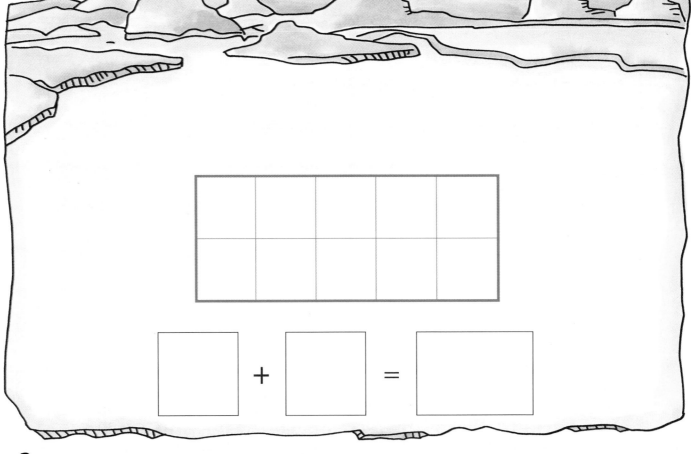

☐ + ☐ = ☐

Notes for Home: Your child told addition stories and recorded one story. *Home Activity:* Ask your child to put 6 raisins in a bag, put in more to make 10, and then write the number sentence.

Act out.

Write.

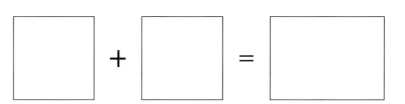

☐ + ☐ = ☐

Notes for Home: Your child used Snap Cubes or counters to act out addition stories, then recorded one story on the page. *Home Activity:* Ask your child to act out a story to show 2 + 7.

Act out. Write.

◻ + ◻ = ◻

◻ + ◻ = ◻

◻ + ◻ = ◻

◻ + ◻ = ◻

Circle.

Draw.

Notes for Home: Your child recorded subtraction stories about groups of 5 lizards or less.
Home Activity: Show your child a group of 5 pennies. Take two away, and ask your child to to tell how many are left.

Name _____

Subtract from 6 and 7

6
in all

2
leave

4
are left

in all

leave

are left

 Notes for Home: Your child told subtraction stories for groups of 6 and 7 and used numbers to show the stories. *Home Activity:* Ask your child to make a group of 6 small objects, and then take 1 away. How many are left?

Write.

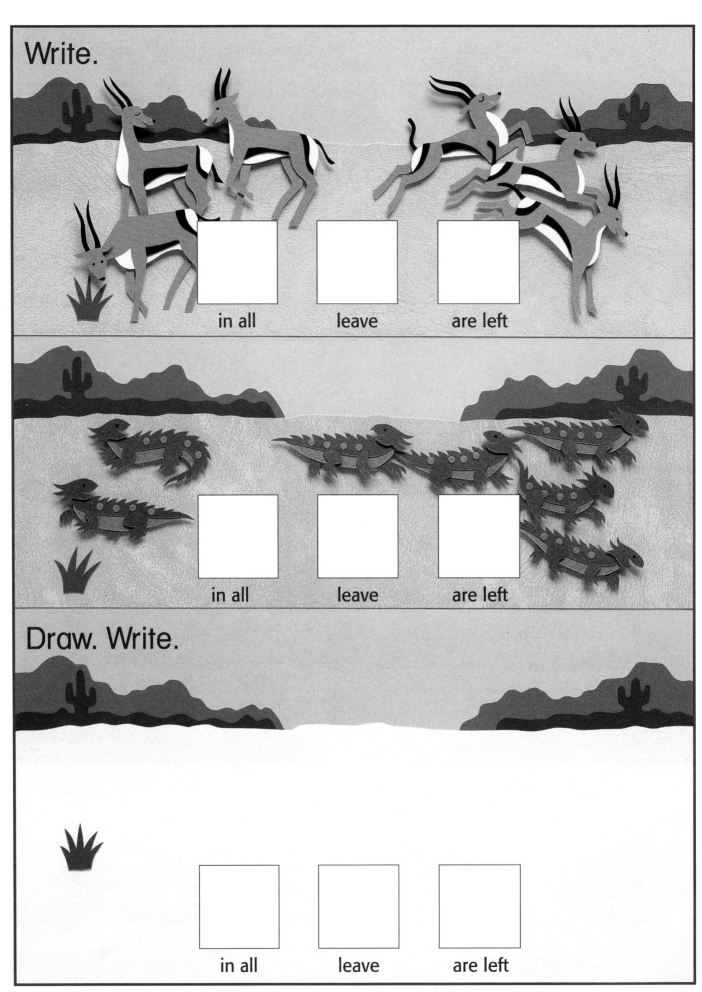

in all   leave   are left

in all   leave   are left

Draw. Write.

in all   leave   are left

Notes for Home: Your child told subtraction stories and wrote numbers to show the stories.
Home Activity: Draw 7 circles and then cover up 2. How many are left?

Subtract from 8 and 9

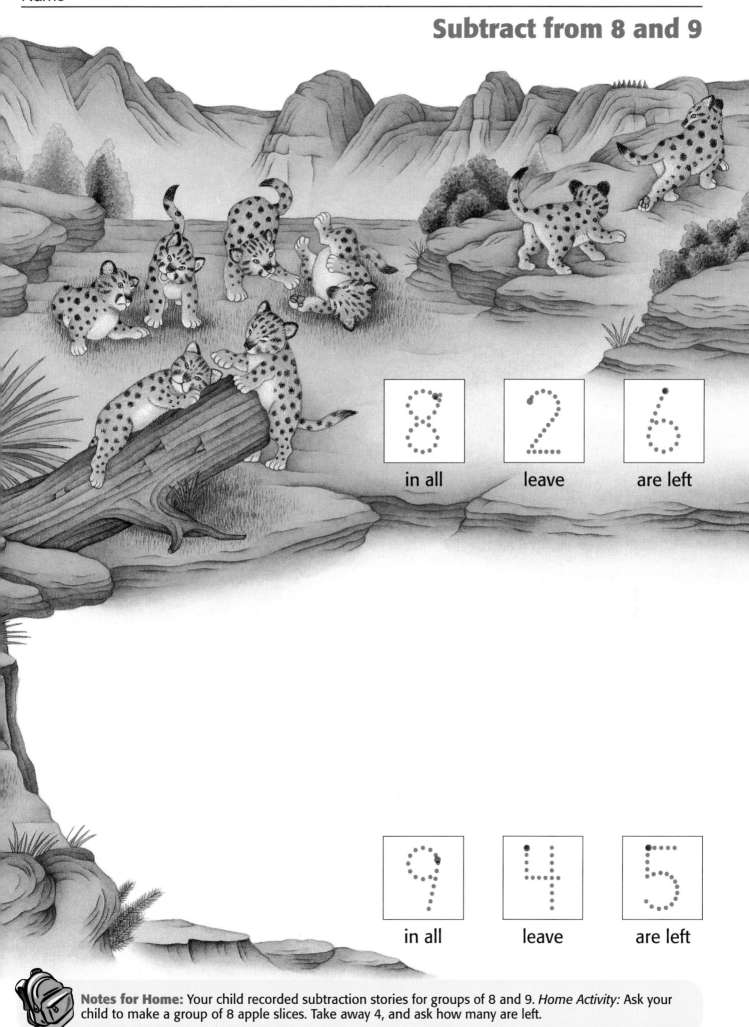

8	2	6
in all	leave	are left

9	4	5
in all	leave	are left

Notes for Home: Your child recorded subtraction stories for groups of 8 and 9. *Home Activity:* Ask your child to make a group of 8 apple slices. Take away 4, and ask how many are left.

Draw. Write.

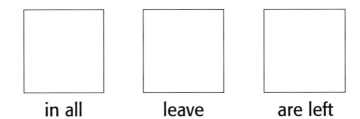

in all   leave   are left

Name _____

Write.

$$10 - 4 = 6$$

Draw. Write.

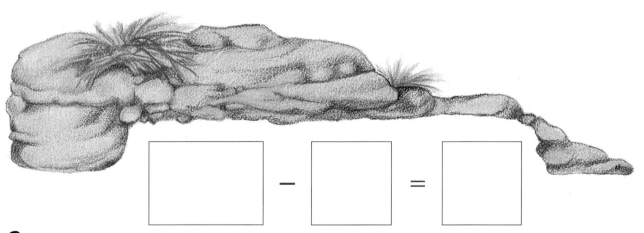

$$\boxed{} - \boxed{} = \boxed{}$$

Notes for Home: Your child drew a picture of a subtraction story and wrote a subtraction sentence to reflect it. *Home Activity:* Ask your child to use 10 beans to act out a subtraction story.

Write.

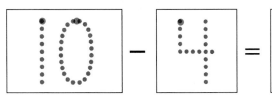

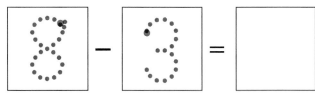

 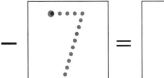 

Notes for Home: Have your child tell a subtraction story for each picture and write the number sentences. *Home Activity:* Ask your child to take 10 snack items, eat some, and then tell how many are left.

298   two hundred ninety-eight

Name

Problem Solving: Choose the Operation

Listen. Circle. Write.

3 ◯ 2 = ☐ ⊕ +
−

9 ◯ 3 = ☐ + −

6 ◯ 4 = ☐ + −

Notes for Home: Your child listened to stories, then chose whether to add or subtract to solve each problem. *Home Activity:* Ask your child to explain what is different about adding and subtracting 2 groups of objects.

Listen. Circle. Write.

6 ◯ 3 = □ ⊕ −

8 ◯ 2 = □ + −

Notes for Home: Your child listened to a story, chose whether to add or subtract, and solved the problem. *Home Activity:* Ask your child to tell when to use + and when to use −.

Chapter 12 Review/Test

Write.

☐ and ☐ is ☐

Draw. Write.

☐ + ☐ = ☐

Notes for Home: Your child wrote numbers and drew a picture to show an understanding of addition. *Home Activity:* Ask your child to tell a number story for 6 + 4 = 10.

Write.

in all   leave   are left

Write.

☐ − ☐ = ☐

Write.

☐ ◯ ☐ ⊜ ☐   + −

Notes for Home: Your child wrote numbers to show an understanding of subtraction and chose addition or subtraction to solve a problem. *Home Activity:* Ask your child to act out a story for 8 − 4.

Animal Faces

What You Need

Paper Plates   Crayons   Art Supplies

What You Do

1

Make an animal face.

2

Cut holes for eyes.

3

Wear the mask.
Act out a story.

Fold down

MathSurf

Scott Foresman - Addison Wesley   My Math Magazine   No. 12

Animal Talk

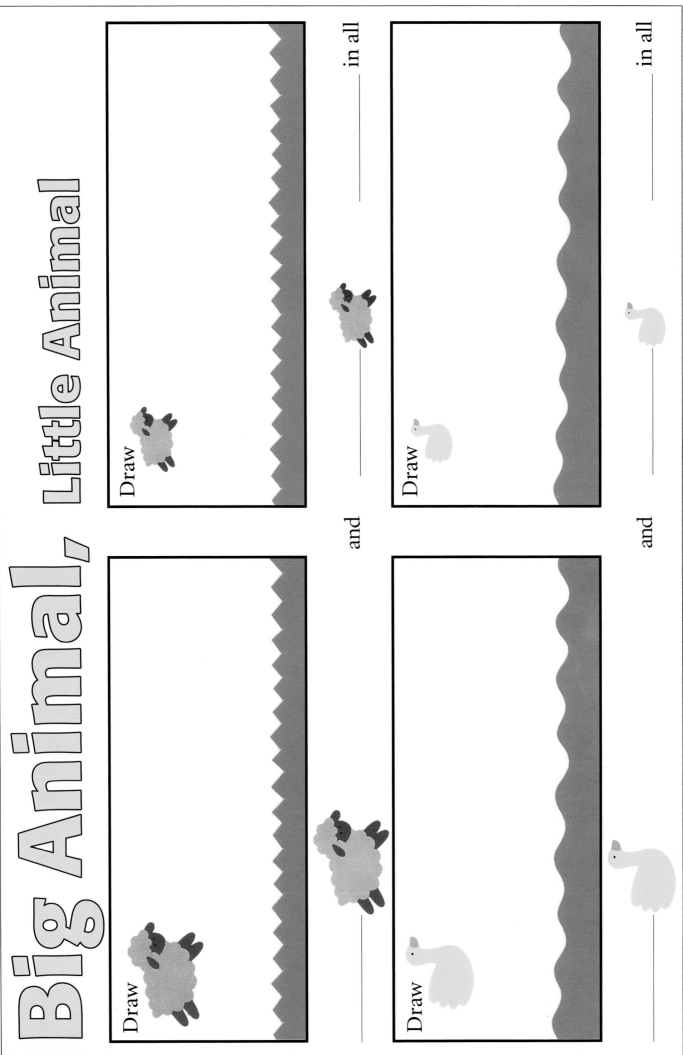

Big Animal, Little Animal

Math Fun

Draw

Draw

and _____ in all

Draw

Draw

and _____ in all

Notes for Home: Your child drew pictures to practice addition.
Home Activity: Using up to 10 toothpicks, help your child join one group to another and say the number sentence to describe the action.

2

Dear Teacher,

This summer, I collected

I found most of them here:

In all, I have ___.

This book tells all about it.

Enjoy,

Summertime Math Fun

Getting Ready for Next Year

Draw.

How many of these?

Draw.

How many of these?

Dear Family,

This booklet encourages your child to collect things over the summer and in the process to practice some basic math skills.

Page 3 gives ideas about what to collect. Your child should draw a picture here of what he or she decides it will be.

Together, pages 4 and 5 form a workmat to use for counting, sorting, finding out how many in all (adding), and how many are left (subtracting). Work together to explore the different ways to use this page to learn facts about your child's collection.

Your child can use pages 6 and 7 to record facts about the collection. It's best to do these pages at the end of the summer when your child's collection is complete.

Page 8 is a letter for your child's new teacher. Your child can finish the letter and take it to school on the first day.

About My _____

How many do I have in all?

How many different kinds?

Draw.

How many of these?

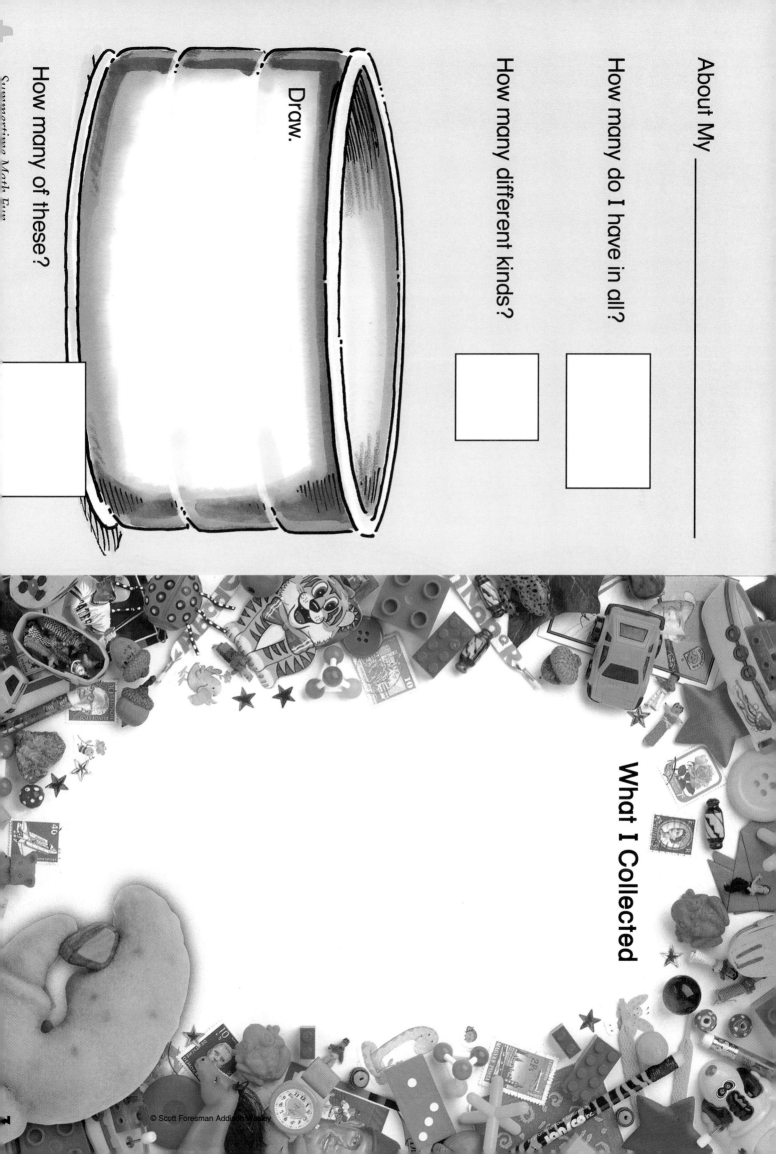

What I Collected

Credits

Illustration

Banek, Yvette 119, 120, 125, 126, 158, 177, 178, 264, 269

Barberi, Sue 84

Barner, Bob 301, 302

Barnum-Newman, Winifred 217, 218

Berrett, Lisa 11, 12, 172, 173, 219, 220, 222, 245, 246, 252, 299, 300

Blasius, Diane 297, 298

Boddy, Joe 229, 230

Brooks, Nan 67, 77, 78

Buchart, Greta 81

Callen, Liz 31

Carpenter, Stephen 122

Chewning, Randy 247, 248

Chung, Chi 295, 296

Clerk, Jessica 209, 210, 229

Cody, Brian 53, 57, 201, 202, 291, 292

Cole, Mernie 183, 184, 192, 255, 261, 283, 284

Colrus, Bill 107, 108, 257, 258

Dieterichs, Shelley 15

DiVito, Anna 163, 227, 271, 272

Dolobowsky, Mena 44, 75, 113, 114, 181, 274

Donohue, Dorothy 19

Dundee, Angela 35, 36, 63, 147, 148

Durrell, Julie 7, 8, 61, 62, 91, 92, 109, 207

Elliot, Gloria 25

Freeman, Nancy 129

Galkin, Simon 17, 18, 239, 240, 252

Gill, Madelaine 1, 289, 290

Goldman, Dara 29, 30, 56, 59, 80, 93, 118, 153, 281, 282

Gordon, Adam 27, 41, 52, 61, 62, 164

Griesbach, Cheryl / Martucci, Stanley 279

Henry, Steve 25, 187, 188, 189, 190, 203

Hirashima, Jean 249, 250

Inouye, Carol 47, 221

Iosa, Ann 5, 6, 85, 191, 276, 285, 286

Jones, Mary 22, 76

Koontz, Robin 33, 34, 110

Kovalik, Terry 69

Levine, Andy 90, 146

Lustig, Loretta 141, 142

Mach, Steven 168

Martinot, Claude 287, 288

McEntire, Larry 121, 243, 244

Mellet-Berry, Fanny 136

Miller, Sue 155, 156, 211, 212

Moffatt, Judy 195, 293, 294

Morse, Deborah 233, 235, 236, 251

Nazz, James 181

O'Malley, Kevin 213

Ovresat, Laura 9, 86,

Paterson, Diane 13, 14

Petrone, Valeria 50, 89, 111, 112

Raymond, Victoria 153

Rockwell, Barry 38, 97

Roth, Roger 137

Schrier, Fred 193, 194, 259, 260

Sharp, Paul 39, 40, 88, 223, 224

Shein, Bob 1, 20, 143, 144, 175

Shepherd, Roni 262, 267, 270, 275

Shola, Georgia 185, 186, 203, 210, 228, 255, 263, 265

Stites, Joe 60, 72, 82, 83, 158, 214, 237, 238

Stuart, Don 49

Swan, Susan 169, 170, 233

Tagel, Peggy 55, 58

Terrill, David 266

Thompson, Emily 64, 138, 176

Tufts, N. Jo 21, 27, 32, 42, 43, 131, 132, 157, 162, 174, 209, 223, 224, 241, 242, 251, 263

Valley, Gregg 3, 4, 10, 139, 140

Veno, Joe 51, 225, 226

Vitsky, Sally 67

Weidner, Bea 207

Weissman, Bari 71, 97, 103, 105, 196

Williams, Toby 97, 99, 100, 106

Math Soup Illustration

Chapter 1
Miller, Susan 2, 3
Shola, George 1

Chapter 2
Davick, Linda 1, 2, 3, 4

Chapter 3
Hine, Eileen 1, 2, 3

Chapter 4
Berry, Holly 2, 3

Chapter 5
Steiger, Terri 1, 2, 3

Chapter 6
Stuart, Don 2, 3

Chapter 7
Grossman, Myron 1, 2, 3

Chapter 8
Westcott, Nadine Bernard 1, 2, 3

Chapter 9
Carter, Abby 1, 2, 3

Chapter 10
Tagel, Peggy 1, 2, 3

Chapter 11
Petrone, Valeria 2, 3

Chapter 12
Tagel, Peggy 2, 3

Photography

Studio photography created expressly for Scott Foresman - Addison Wesley by Richard Hutchings and Tony Holmes, with the exception of Math Soup which was photographed by Fritz Geiger and Michael Walker.

Cover Japack/Westlight

Math Soup Photography

Chapter 11
Courtesy Cheryl Henson and the Muppet Workshop™, Jim Henson Productions, Inc. 1

Summertime Math Fun

Cover Maass, Mary Kumick

Lustig, Loretta 3-4
Stites, Joe 1, 6-7
Stuart, Don 8

Workmat 2

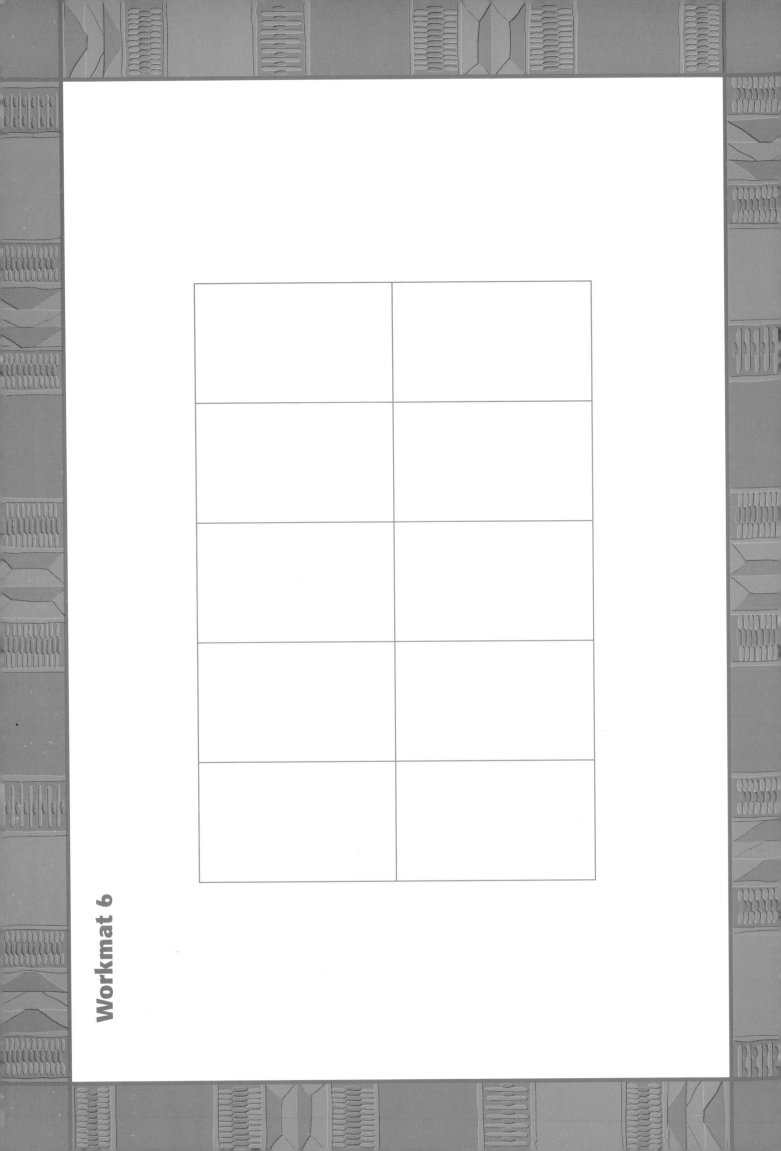

Workmat 6